Israel Abrahams, Claude Goldsmid Montefiore

Aspects of Judaism being sixteen sermons

Israel Abrahams, Claude Goldsmid Montefiore

Aspects of Judaism being sixteen sermons

ISBN/EAN: 9783744745178

Printed in Europe, USA, Canada, Australia, Japan

Cover: Foto ©Lupo / pixelio.de

More available books at **www.hansebooks.com**

ASPECTS OF JUDAISM

BEING

Sixteen Sermons

BY

ISRAEL ABRAHAMS
AND
CLAUDE G. MONTEFIORE

London
MACMILLAN AND CO
AND NEW YORK
1895

PREFACE.

The Sermons contained in this volume, with three exceptions, were all delivered at various Jewish religious services. Though there is no basis in Jewish history for a distinction between clergy and laity, in practice such a distinction inevitably arose towards the end of the middle-ages. Yet, laymen though we are, and though our opinions on many points may not be generally shared by Jews, we have nevertheless been permitted to occupy the pulpit in several Jewish places of worship. This fact is not merely a source of gratification to ourselves, but seems to speak well for the liberality of modern Judaism.

The views of the Jewish religion taken by the two contributors to this small book are in themselves not altogether identical. We feel, however, that over and above the bond of friendship and of common literary work, there is sufficient consistency of teaching to justify the two sets of sermons being included within the same covers. We ought perhaps to add that neither of us has been at pains, in revising his sermons, to force absolute consistency even in his own individual views. Our words have been spoken at irregular intervals, extending over many years; and there may probably be some diversities of tone and thought between one sermon and the next.

We are fully conscious that our ideas are often tentative, and yet we hope there is some constructiveness as well. Doubtless the subjects chosen were frequently beyond our powers, but our imperfect and halting treatment of them has fulfilled, as we believe, one requisite at least, and therefore to this single merit we may lay claim. We have written honestly and without reserve. We have expressed our full selves and extenuated nothing. If it be found that our faith in Judaism, as we conceive it, has sometimes clouded our judgment, we can but reply that this faith constitutes the only plea of justification for the present volume.

CONTENTS.

PART I.

BY ISRAEL ABRAHAMS.

		PAGE
I.	FRIENDSHIP	1
II.	ANGELS	15
III.	THE OPEN DOOR	29
IV.	A NEW SONG	42
V.	THE LOVE OF MAN	56
VI.	THE NEGATIVE FORM OF THE GOLDEN RULE	66
VII.	THE LOVE OF GOD	78
VIII.	THE HATRED OF EVIL	93

PART II.

By CLAUDE G. MONTEFIORE.

		PAGE
I.	The Omnipresence of God	107
II.	Holiness	125
III.	Religious Liberty	144
IV.	"Ye are my Witnesses"	163
V.	The Contemplation of Death	183
VI.	The Way of Righteousness	205
VII.	Religion and Morality	222
VIII.	The Consciousness of Judaism	241

ON FRIENDSHIP.

"Either Friendship or Death!"

These pathetic words are applied in the Talmud[1] to a certain Choni Hameagel, the man who, in the legend, fell asleep for seventy years, and when he awoke found the world around him changed, the old familiar faces gone, and himself without comrades. "Give me friendship or give me death!" he prayed. And God heard him, and he died.

It is curious to notice the varying degrees of interest which different ages feel regarding important matters of social philosophy. A case very much in point may be found in the subject of friendship. Classical philosophers like Plato[2] and Cicero, Jewish moralists like the

---

[1] *Taanith*, p. 23.
[2] Cf. Jowett's Introduction to the *Lysis*.

author of the Book of Ecclesiasticus, were fond of discussing the meaning, the conditions, and the claims of friendship. But in modern times very little has been written, and less has been thought, about it. Yet the subject of friendship is of great practical moment both for life and for religion; and the neglect of the subject as a matter of discussion has, perhaps, led to its neglect as a matter of conduct.

Now, many men and women suffer acutely, especially in their later years, because they have made no friendships, or have lost those that they once had made. For what does friendship mean? "A friend," says Emerson, "is a person with whom I may be sincere; before him I may think aloud." The Rabbis said the same thing. "Get a companion," they counsel us, "to whom you can tell all your secrets."[1] See how this cuts both ways. To a friend you reveal your entire self, but if so, it cannot be an altogether bad self. You would be ashamed to lay bare to your friend an ugly heart, and so your

---

[1] *Aboth de R. Nathan,* viii.

very friendship forces you to make your heart fair. The surest safeguard against conceit, against selfishness, against petty vindictiveness, against all the lesser vices, is to have a friend to whom you must tell everything, before whom you not only may, but must think aloud. Many men would be better men, certainly they would be happier men, if they knew how to think aloud, and to think nothing that they would not reveal.

I said that many of us suffer because we make no friends. But is this, you will say, the right phrase to use? Can one *make* friends? True, some are in the happy circumstance that their friendships are born to them. They take our hearts by storm, or rather our hearts surrender to them at discretion. Such are the darlings of fortune: they have inherited the priceless wealth of sunny smiles and of overflowing love. These are the friendly beings who love everyone and everything, and are loved in return by everyone and everything. But most of us are not of this blessed species. Our friendships do not come to us; they must be sought. And the ways of modern life have much to answer for. Our current habits destroy the conditions of friendship. Old friendly habits are going; and friendship can only grow in a soil of friendly habit. Even at the risk of being charged with harping for ever on one string, I can never help lamenting that so much of its cameraderie has gone out of Jewish life. Once upon a time each Jewish congregation was one big family; the members were all interested in one another. Mind, we have kept some of the old traits. We are still inquisitive about one another; we peep and pry into one another's affairs; we read the front page of the *Jewish Chronicle* with laudable curiosity. But why does this curiosity stop short of friendliness? Because our interest in one another is languid, is only simulated; the genuine friendliness has been killed by our dropping one by one the good old Jewish customs which converted inquisitiveness into love. I am thinking, remember, rather of social than of religious customs. When a man was newly wed in olden times, the whole congregation sang to him in synagogue the chapter in Genesis describing how Isaac's marriage was made in heaven, and expressed the hope that the new union would prove thus divinely blessed. It was a friendly God-speed; but now, when a man is "called up," in our synagogues, as a bridegroom, we confer on him a momentary stare. And in the good old days, again, the whole atmosphere of Jewish life was made friendly by the concern which each Jew felt in all Jews' children. As every year the Feast of Weeks came round, each tiny boy, just as soon as he was able to lisp his Hebrew alphabet, was carried to the synagogue; he was put in the Rabbi's arms, and the Rabbi bent down over the child and kissed him, and gave him a cake on which was inscribed in honey the verse, "The Law which Moses commanded unto us is the inheritance of the house of Jacob," and the child lisped the words after him, sucked the honey and ate the cake, that the words of the Law might be sweet in his mouth, and all the congregation beamed with smiles. Such habits as these were small matters, were they not—trifles, and rather insignificant? But these habits, as I said, generated a warm atmosphere of love, while now we have raised a cold cloud of indifference, even of mutual contempt. I am not preaching a reactionary doctrine; I am not one of those who would see Judaism stand still; nay, I am for change and progress in many directions. But why should progress divorce itself from poetry? why should it be a just taunt that the tendency is to make Judaism, as it progresses, ever more unlovely, ever more unloveable?

It is a serious matter, for it is mostly in loving environments that friendships arise. You focus your overflowing affections, you concentrate the stream. But you cannot do this unless you start with a general stock of affectionateness to focus and to concentrate. So we are brought by another road to the answer to my question: Can one *make* real friendships? If they do not come of themselves, is it not vain to court them? To which I answer: Every one can make friendships, and every one ought. All of us can make ourselves likeable if we try hard enough. You can find out your graces, and make the most of them: you can cultivate your flowers, you can pluck out the weeds, you can detect what repels in you and can suppress it. And because one can do this easiest when one is quite young, the best, the most lasting, the most loving friendships are made in youth. Hence fathers and mothers owe it to their children to watch them closely, to contrive that they make friends. If I see a child without friends, I regard it as a very grave symptom, and I blame the parents, not the child. It shows, indeed, that the child is shy or unamiable, but also that the mother is callous and neglectful. When you find your children friendless, look to it; cure the fault and the failing before it is too late. A solitary child makes a one-sided, half-hearted, half-developed man or woman. No mother's subsequent tenderness can compensate for the loss of a child's friendship with a child, nothing can replace the neglected interchange of young confidences. It is the rubbing of one unformed character on another that brings each character to its own highest.

But whether your friendships come in youth or in maturer years, do not attempt to buy them. You may make, but you cannot buy friendships. You may offer gifts and services, but you will not thereby win love. Many people entertain, as they call it, extensively, keep an open table, and spend, perhaps, more than they can afford, but they spread their net in vain. "At the door of the shop," says the Talmudic proverb, "are many friends and comrades; at the gate of grief are neither friends nor comrades;"[1] that is, friends bought by gifts and meals are sunshine and cupboard friends, who cannot weather the storms nor survive the emptying of the larder. True friendship may lead to an exchange of services, but it must not be founded on services, whether mutual or one-sided. The secret of friendship is in being, not in serving; we want from our friends, "not what they have, but what they are." "A faithful friend," says Ecclesiasticus,[2] thinking of the utilitarian aspect of friendship, "is the medicine of life": but then a healthy man does not use medicine every day. He likes to know that

---

[1] Talmud, *Sabbath*, p. 32; cf. Ecclus. vi. 10.
[2] vi. 16.

it is there, but he does not wish to use it often.

Some of us have to buy friendships with gifts, because we have not been trained in youth to win them by friendliness. Some of us feel a passion for friendships when we grow older, when the world looks dark and the clouds of age begin to gather; but we have not learned the art of giving the passion play. And then, not having learnt how to make friends, we rush into the market to buy them. Or, worse still, the effort to buy friends may be due to mere snobbishness. We would have for our friends people whom we think a little bit above us in the social scale. Thus we seek our friends among strangers, not in our own families. I have already said that we need the friendship, even the mere acquaintanceship, of those who are not allied to us in blood; but is that a reason why we should pass over our own relatives in disdain? How many people make friends of their relatives, or confidants even of their brothers? Oh, no; they hide themselves from their own flesh. And they discover, too late, that their family ties are weak; that brothers who played and laughed and cried together, who learned to pray together at their mother's knees, have drifted asunder, far from one another's lives. This miserable neglect has an ample way of revenging itself. Ecclesiasticus asks,[1] "Is it not a grief unto death, when a comrade and friend is turned into an enemy?" Aye, and is it not, I ask, a grief more bitter still, when those who might have been among our surest friends, our own nearest who might have been our dearest, are slighted and estranged, and we are left to lament the absence of that family friendship which might have brightened our lives, doubled our joys, and divided our pains?

And next to the ties of blood in making friendships come those of race and religion. In spite of the better relations between us and the world, the first friends of a Jew are naturally Jews. Ought we to have any others? Is it a prudent or praiseworthy thing for Jews to culti-

---

[1] xxxvii. 2.

vate close, intimate, home friendships with Christians? A difficult question, but I am in no doubt of my own answer. In England you find some Jewish families whose friends are exclusively Christians; but these are the superfine beings who think anything Jewish beneath their lordly notice. And these cases are comparatively few. Comparatively few Jewish families in this metropolis have intimate Christian friends at all—friends who come much to the house, who enter completely into the home circle. In the colonies and in the smaller English towns these intimacies are much more common. In towns like London we seem to have raised round our homes the walls of a voluntary ghetto. It is not easy in a day to recover from the isolation of three centuries. And it is feared that friendships—close, home friendships with Christians—will lead to intermarriage and possible apostasy, or at least to the weakening of the hold of Jews on Judaism. I admit that the risk of intermarriage is real enough. But surely though real, the nature of the risk is entirely misunderstood by us. The effectual barrier to apostasy is heartfelt religious fervour, not artificial social barriers. If you make your home a genuinely Jewish home, you will not endanger your children's fidelity by introducing Christian friends to its most sacred and innermost shrines. Some notorious mixed marriages have occurred in Jewish families whence Christian friends were rigidly excluded. Again, some of the best Jews I know were brought up almost entirely with Christian friends, because they lived in places where there were no Jews. I do not deny that they lost by the want of Jewish intercourse, but others lose more by restricting themselves to Jewish intercourse. The moral gains derived of comradeship with people of another faith are quite incalculable. The Jew and the Christian bring to each other just those elements of unlikeness which give piquancy to friendship; they round off each other's angles; they introduce each other to a fresh view of the world; they each show to each how narrow and uninspiring his own horizon becomes when he confines his gaze to one set of scenes, to one series of colours. Jews and Christians will never understand one another until they are freely admitted to each other's home circles, until they are received into the sacred bonds of friendship. But it is hard to lay down general rules on this very debateable question. "Bring not every one into your house," says Ecclesiasticus;[1] and some of you may think his counsel truer than mine. But, though nice discrimination may be needed in the matter, let us at least face the question honestly. Our boys and girls go to Christian schools, where budding friendships arise which, a generation ago, were not present even in germ. The problem is thus a new one, and every Jewish mother must face the question fairly and squarely, whether these friendships ought to be killed in the bud, as they so commonly are killed at present. Of this I am nearly certain: though many Christians feel a repugnance against these friendships with Jews, yet the main, the most persistent, objections are raised from our side.

---

[1] xi. 29.

Let us, however, quit this doubtful point, and close with a certainty. The author of the Book of Proverbs says: "Keep thy heart with all diligence, for out of it are the issues of life."[1] It must not pass without notice that, in our Jewish liturgy, we pray every morning to God to give us true friends, to keep us far from evil companionship.[2] For a man's friends make him or mar him. Therefore, diligently guard your hearts. Open them not to every one; yet he is a foolish sentinel who shuts the gate of his fortress to friends lest a foe perchance slip in. Be jealous of your hearts; teach them to discriminate; but, above all, teach them to love. God, the Friend of friends, will send His grace unto you, and, instead of Choni Hameagel's despairing cry, "Either Friendship or Death," your hopeful choice will be, "Friendship and Life."

---

[1] iv. 23.

[2] *Authorised Daily Prayer Book*, ed. Rev. S. Singer, p. 7.

ANGELS.

"For he shall give his angels charge over thee, to keep thee in all thy ways." [1]

THERE are some thoughts which preserve their dainty freshness only so long as they are left unexpressed. If you put certain poetical fancies into words, still more if you attempt a pictorial representation of them, you run the risk of doing like the collector, who catches a butterfly and pins it to a card in his cabinet. He transforms a living loveliness into a scientific skeleton. Sometimes we are apt to regret that there is no such thing as religious art in Judaism, that the second commandment prevented Jewish artists from seeking to realise in colours or in marble the supernatural scenes

---

[1] Psalms xci. 11.

and poetical conceptions of Scripture. Less beautiful than it might otherwise have been in externals, Judaism has remained simpler and truer in essence. Our religion has not altogether lost by the absence of the glowing ornaments which the skill of painters has devised to beautify so many Catholic places of worship. This thought seems to me specially applicable to the case of Angels. An Angel ought to have wings, for flying is the perfection of rapid and graceful motion; bird-like the Angel is now visible, now invisible, as it moves. But when one sees a picture of an incongruous winged being, with pinions that hardly seem to belong to it, the religious conception that is embodied in the notion of an Angel is lost in a certain sense of the ludicrous. Beautiful as Correggio's Angels are, we can spare even such figures from our Synagogue ceilings.

But I shall be told that though I deride these pictorial representations, still one must have some idea what an Angel looks like. How would you tell an Angel if you were to meet one? My friends, it is not everybody who has the gift of recognising an Angel at once. In Bible times,[1] Angels sometimes came and people did not know them at first sight. Besides, the Angels are not all alike: and if you ask, how do Angels look? I can but answer that it depends on who is looking at them, and in what frame of mind.

To Abraham, the hospitable entertainer of travellers, the three Angels came as weary wayfarers;[2] to Jacob, who from his birth onward had to battle against adverse fate, the Angel came as an antagonist to wrestle with him.[3] Moses, destined to bring new light to illumine the old dim-eyed world, saw his Angel in the bright burning bush.[4] Joshua, the bold warrior-chief, with thoughts on victory intent, met his Angel under the form of an armed man; before whom the hero did not quail, but fanatically brave demanded: "Art thou for us or for our adversaries?"[5] David, however, *did* quail when he saw the destroying Angel's sword

---

[1] Genesis xviii. 1.   [2] Ibid.   [3] Genesis xxxii. 24.
[4] Exodus iii. 2.   [5] Joshua v. 13.

directed against Jerusalem, for alas! he had sinned, and conscience made a coward of him, but even in that strait his heroic unselfishness came to his help.[1] Tobiah, eager and young, anxious to start off to seek his fortunes, finds his Angel as a radiant youth, who is ready for an immediate start, but in truth has a mission of healing to perform, and his name is "God's Healer."[2] Heliodorus, greedy for gold, came to despoil the Maccabean Temple, but an Angel approached in the shape of a prancing horse completely harnessed in gold, which with his fore-feet struck down the covetous robber.[3] Throughout the Maccabean period men saw Angels on every side as armed men, and beheld warriors in the sky,[4] for they themselves were warlike. When, after the Roman destruction of the State, the valour of the Jews cooled, and they no longer dreamed of recovering their independence by force of arms, they met Angels in the form of

---

[1] 2 Samuel xxiv. 17.   [2] Tobit v. 4.
[3] 2 Maccabees iii. 25.   [4] Ibid. v. 2-3.

Elijah,[1] the type of the national intensity and energy, yet withal himself unarmed. And so these Angels put on their various forms, for the most part nameless, but their name was Wonder!—nameless, *i.e.*, until after the Babylonian exile, when Persian influence gave names and numbers to Jewish Angels. As time went on, the Angels changed with it. Philo, the noble-minded Alexandrian Jew, thought that God would not have created this imperfect world without some intermediate agency; so the Angels appeared to him as these intermediate agencies. To Maimonides,[2] the philosopher, the Angels came as philosophers, as incorporeal intelligences, creative forces that act unseen, beings that participate in the divine essence, but are not co-eternal with God, the souls of the spheres which make music as they roll. The Mystics, on the other hand, being fantastic poets, saw strange and awful beings as the

---

[1] Many passages in the Talmudic literature, based on Malachi iv. 5.

[2] *Guide of the Perplexed*, Part II., ch. vi.

Angels of their cloud-dreams. Maimonides spiritualised the Angels, till they were too fine for ordinary thought, and thus many of them died; the Kabbalists, or Jewish Mystics, materialised the Angels, until they became too gross to live. The Metatoron of the Mystics became a sort of little god, a subordinate deity, and we must be grateful that they did at least make him subordinate.[1] Gradually the Synagogue has been abandoning its mysticism; the Kabbala holds but a feeble sway. With this change some of our poetry, alas! goes also. In some Hebrew prayer-books you still may read an invocation for the official who sounds the shofar, or ram's horn, on the New Year's festival; you may read how he used to appeal to the Angel set over the Shofar; how each particular note of the horn had its own particular Angel to carry it on high; how Angels went in with the blower's breath at one end and Angels came out with the sounds at the

---

[1] See Graetz, *History of the Jews* (English translation), vol. iii., p. 156.

other. Ay, it would need strong imaginative power nowadays to hear angelic voices in the notes of the Shofar, when blown by some shrill producer of discords. Yet, if there is some spiritual danger, there is also beauty, there is permanent life in the thought that these countless myriads of Angels hover around us, ready to assume a bright or dark aspect, according as our thoughts are bright or dark; coming to each one of us, as friend or foe, according to our deserts, dressed to suit the temperature of our own hearts; carrying our message to God on the wings of the wind; guarding us in all our ways, lest, perchance, we dash our foot against a stone.

No, my friends, the Angels are not yet dead; and some of them come to earth, and dwell in our midst. They still have no distinguishing names; they may be quite ordinary in appearance, not always beautiful or graceful; they may be quite unromantic and matter of fact, for they may be simple human beings, serving God and serving men on God's behalf. Perhaps this is why, except in a doubtful vision of Zechariah, no Angels in the Bible ever assumed the female form, and all the Biblical Angels are men. Woman's angelic mission was to be unobtrusive, ministering to those that suffer. She needs no other cloak than her womanliness, no other wings than her swift sensitiveness, her quick sympathy. When Abraham was about to slay Isaac, the Angels in the legend[1] wept sorrowful tears, which fell on Isaac's neck, hardening it and rendering it innocuous to the blow. How often since have women's tears softened the strokes directed against the hearts of those they love, healing the wounds that they could not prevent!

But if we would ensure the continued presence of the Angels among us, we must imitate others of their qualities besides their sympathy. Sympathy alone is not enough to save; sympathy must be concentrated. "One Angel," say the Rabbis, "has only one mission at a time."[2] The world might be a fitter place for Angels' visits if we possessed something of this

---

[1] *Genesis Rabba*, § 56. [2] Ibid., § 50.

angelic concentration, if our sympathies were less diffuse and therefore stronger, if we gave our hearts more fully to our fellows, if our conceit did not render us so anxious to have a *finger* in everything, while we have a *hand* in nothing. Then, again, has it ever struck you how chary the Angels were of their words? The Angels of the Bible did many wonderful things, but they had very little to say. They mostly speak in monosyllables; they rarely utter two sentences together, and when they have done their work they go, without waiting for thanks. Imagine a would-be human Angel setting about, say, the rescue of Hagar from the wilderness to-day. He would call a public meeting, elect himself chairman of a committee of ways and means; he would bore everyone to death with eloquent speeches, and he would send some one else to the spot just too late to save her, whereupon he would receive a hearty vote of thanks for his prompt philanthropy. We carry this policy into our prayers at this season of the year, when the Day of Atonement is near at hand. We call public meetings in the synagogues; lengthily and lustily we confess in words that we are sinners, and expect I know not what from our condescension. Yet men's words create no Angels; but, say the Rabbis, men's honest acts do. "Every deed well done gives birth to an Angel who watches over the doer."[1] Isaiah's Angels had but one voice to speak with, and six wings to fly with and to act. What an angelic world this would be if every one of us did six times as much as he said!

The Angels, however, were not perfect. Sometimes they quarrelled, and formed parties in heaven. So God put away far from Him the Angels of strife, and kept near His throne only those whose mission was peace.[2] If God is angry with men, He summons the wrathful Angel from His remote resting place; and perchance the sinner may repent before the angry Angel arrives. Peace with rapid flight, with strong and tense wings; anger slow to move and heavy of gait! So in our hearts, too, may

---

[1] *Exodus Rabba*, § 32.
[2] Midrash *Tehillim*, ch. lxxxvi.

love be near and ready, hate far off and unprepared. The Angels in the Rabbinical legends are strangely human; sometimes they show jealousy of man, sometimes contempt for him. Now they plead for him, again they ask: "What is man that Thou rememberest him?" Sometimes they would destroy him, sometimes they love to assume his form. This mixture of fire and water, as the Rabbi puts it,[1] in the angelic character, is the most intensely human thing of all. Angels have their inconsistencies, and men are like Angels when the fire of their enthusiasm for good struggles against their cold indifference. It is not a superhuman task to make the fire prevail. There were, says the Talmud, Angels born for a day, for a purpose, for a special need; and when that day was passed, that purpose accomplished, that need supplied, the Angels vanished into the spirit stream from which they temporarily emerged, to be, if need were, revived for further work.[2] Is

---

[1] Talmud of Jerusalem, Rosh Hashanah, ch. ii.
[2] *Exodus Rabba*, § 15.

it impossible for us to be thus angelically active for a day, for a purpose, for a special need ? Is our day so very long that we must weary of trying before the night come ? Or worse, shall we pretend to deceive our neighbours, perhaps deceiving ourselves, forgetful that our imposture will be found out, at least when the night comes ? These false angels dress for the part accurately enough. They put on sham wings, but like those of Icarus, the wings fall off when put to the test of flying ; they deck their heads with imitation aureoles ; they sing lip-praises to God; they raise themselves on their feet towards one another, and cry, "Holy! Holy! Holy!" like any Angel of the heavenly choir. Strip them of this angelic garniture which they put on once a year, and you betray them. Nay, my friends, to be an Angel for a day one must be an Angel for a year, but each day's effort makes the next day's easier. David's magic harp that hung over his bed would not, while the King slept, have given forth sweet music whenever the wind touched the strings, unless David, when awake, had kept the harp constantly in tune. Constancy alone produces automatic sensitiveness to the touch of virtue. In Psalm lxxviii., manna is called "Angels' food," yet the Israelites at first disliked the manna in the wilderness; again and again they clamoured for other food. It took forty long years to sweeten it to their taste, to fit their palates for the gift of Angels' food. And this extended effort, this long drawn-out trial of the race which bore God's light for the world, became an eternal exemplar of the angelic work that men may perform.

Familiar with all the languages that come from the tortured heart, for Gabriel knew all the tongues of men,[1] our prophets and our priests were called Angels.[2] "Who are ministering Angels?" asked a Talmudist, and he answered, "The Rabbis."[3] The winds and the lightning, the trees and the rain, everything that stirs or breathes, everything that lifelessly rests, these are God's Angels doing His work, obeying

---

[1] Talmud, Sota, p. 33.   [2] Malachi ii. 7.
[3] Kiddushin, p. 72a.

His will. Yes, God's Angels are with us, and He has given them charge over us to protect us in all our ways. We have our Michaels, our Angels of judgment and power; our Gabriels, men of God, comforters; our Raphaels, healers from God, to cure body and soul; we have our Uriels, who, lighted by the fire of God, pursue truth whithersoever it lead them. Still may Israel place himself amid the guardian Angels who keep the way of the tree of life; the tree of Judaism, whose leaves change with the seasons, but whose roots are fixed for ever, drawing moisture from a never-failing spring. And when we have each to leave this earthly scene, when we must transfer the charge to those that survive us, may the summoning angel come not as an Angel of Death, but as an Angel of Life, gently saying, "Thy day is over, but fear not, for thy work is done. Still has God given His Angels charge over thee, to keep thee in all thy ways."

"THE OPEN DOOR."[1]

"I opened to my beloved; but my beloved had withdrawn himself and was gone; my soul had failed me when he spake; I sought him, but I could not find him; I called him, but he gave me no answer."[2]

IT was at midday on the anniversary of the present festival—the Passover—that Abraham, according to Jewish legend,[3] was seated at the door of his tent eagerly scanning the horizon in search of a possible guest. The patriarch was ill and feeble, but the good God, desirous of sparing him, had caused Gehinom itself to belch forth its fires to add to the stifling heat of the

---

[1] This sermon was delivered in Passover (April), 1890, when there was much discussion in the Anglo-Jewish community concerning some necessary ritual reforms.

[2] Song of Songs, v. 6.

[3] Midrash, *Tanchuma* to Exodus, xii. 41, etc.

sun, and the surface of the earth was so dry and the air so sultry that no wayfarer could venture to journey on. Everyone had turned aside to seek shelter and shade. But Abraham became uneasy. His generous heart was sorely pained at the thought that none was nigh to enter his door. He sent Eleazar his servant to look around, but his search was fruitless. Still unsatisfied, Abraham, weak though he was, himself rose to see with his own eyes whether any one was perchance at hand; when, behold, hard by the Oak of Mamre shone the glory of God, and three men were near to enter his tent. These, though he knew it not, were three angelic messengers of healing and hope.

A happy instinct, this, to associate with the Passover the longing of the patriarch to gather all comers into his hospitable tent without asking them any questions. For the Passover commemorates the first stage in the history of that race that was destined to give the world its law of religion and morality—to maintain in word and deed the brotherhood of man. But since the time of Abraham, even since the date of the foregoing legend, the world has not progressed very rapidly in learning this lesson. Sometimes it seems as though succeeding ages devoted their energies to unlearning as quickly as might be what had already been acquired. The modern world has become more civilised, but it has had to pay the price. One of the first marks of civilisation is to shut one's door against one's fellow-man. The Bedouin and the savage may dare to keep open tent; the first rough settlers in a new colony do not know what it is to deny entrance to a stranger. In an English village people may sleep secure with unlocked doors. But so surely as men congregate in towns—wherein civilisation makes itself a home—so surely they do *not* leave their doors open to all comers. No doubt prudence dictates this course; but prudence does not justify it all. For you may love and warmly love without overmuch fear of thieves if *you* are honest; and our suspiciousness, even of brethren in religion and race, our dread of being deceived, of being laughed at for entertaining a knave, leads us to lose Abraham's opportunity of receiving into our houses angels unawares.

There was an old Jewish custom of leaving the street doors open during meals, both as a general thing and in particular on the Passover night. A direct invitation was addressed to passers-by, " All who need, let them join in our Passover; all who are hungry, let them enter and eat." This paragraph was written in Chaldee, because the man in the street would best understand that language in Babylon, where the paragraph was composed. We still invite people to come in, but we take the precaution of not being heard. We shut our doors upon one another, and roar you to enter as gently as any sucking-dove. We keep the Chaldee; because there's no fear of the modern man in the street understanding it. I do not deny that we are as charitable to the poor as ever; we open our purses, but we shut our doors. And I am not thinking primarily or specially of the poor, nor of the material meal with which the table may be spread.

In the later Middle Ages a sort of faint

shadow of the old custom may be caught. It became habitual to open the door on the Passover eve, at the end of the meal. This looks rather inhospitable, but the door was opened for a special guest; for Elijah, the harbinger of the Messiah. His wine cup was ready for him, let him enter and drink of it. A halo of poetry surrounds such customs as these, that originated when the bitterness of suffering intensified the longing hope for Divine intervention. It is almost a pity that the custom never became universal, and that, from an erroneous belief that it had objectionable associations, it is fast dying out even where it had obtained a hold.

In 1442, Pope Eugenius IV. issued a most offensive Bull; he decreed that the Jews should keep their doors and windows shut during the Easter week. He was induced to take this step by the advice of a certain Alonzo, the son of an apostate Jew.[1] About twenty years later

---

[1] Graetz, *History of the Jews* (English translation), vol. iv., p. 271.

the same thing happened in Spain, where our brethren were confined to their houses during the Holy Week at the instigation of Don Pacheco, himself of Jewish descent. These edicts were not isolated, but were frequently repeated. Surely it is bad enough that such barriers should be placed on Jewish intercourse from without, we need not add similar restrictions of our own and against one another. At the table whereat the story of the Exodus is narrated all Jews must be as brothers; and differences on questions of ritual, at best insignificant, must not be permitted to erect a barrier between those united by a common history and a common triumph over misfortune and obloquy. To shut Judaism up within narrow sectarian boundaries is indeed a work best left to apostates; we from within should widen our approaches, and, unlike the Roman augurs, throw open our doors as a symbol of peace with one another and with the world.

Even though we may shut our door on the present, the shadows of the past fall athwart our table on the Seder-night. What a contrasted group of guests[1]—some majestic and noble, others very commonplace; some childlike and quaintly dressed, others hoary and bowed, crowned with a diadem of reverential awe. All the representatives of man's history are there—in the four classes of his children; the son that made for the good, and he that worked for evil; the wise who opens up with bold and independent questioning the world's mysteries; the son who knows not how to ask, to whom nature must of her own accord reveal her secrets. These children are always of our company. And the Rabbis, discoursing of the departure from Egypt; their voices echo in our ears as we catch the soft tones of their once animated talk and are fain to make our whole meal off the crumbs that fell from their table. In the pages of our Seder-book they still discourse, until we, their descendants, mindful of the strange and chequered history that has unrolled itself since those assembled at

---

[1] All the persons mentioned in this paragraph occur in this oldest of all home rites, the *Seder*, or home service, read round the table on the Passover-eve.

Bene Berak lived and died, convinced of the noble mission that links us with the teachers of old—till we too find that the time has come to confess, with the martyred Akiba leading the chorus—Hear, O Israel, the Lord thy God is one! And to us, with many others, comes Rabban Gamaliel, leading by the hand Eleazar the son of Azariah—a grey-haired youth—like the present surmounted by all the wisdom of the ages. Arm-in-arm come Jose the Galilean, scoffed at by fishwives for his birth, but belonging by right to the assembly of the wise, and Tarphon who neglected not his duty, though he said that art was long and time fleeting. And to show that we are not at all exclusive, some far more modern guests grace our table on this night. Kalir, with rugged voice, wanting a little in sweetness, yet powerful and of wide compass, sings to us his ninth-century songs in verses of bold originality, and even a non-Jewish poet decks our board with his fairy garland. Whose form is that, clad in spotless garments, with a gentle, peaceful smile playing o'er a countenance lit up by immeasurable love and calm?

It is Hillel. He is present, too, for in memory of him we to-night mix our unleavened bread and bitter herbs, and thus partake concurrently of the bitter-sweets of freedom. But calm lasts not for ever, and a stormy guest is with us also. Not in person, not even in distinct memory, but as the shadow of a shade. Elijah the storm-compelling, rudely dressed, mighty of will, and energetic to fight for the Lord. Nay, he cometh not to-night, though his cup be ready, and here and there the door be open to admit him. But what though he come not to-night, what though he come not at all? Yet can we make his coming sure and near, for each, by opening his own heart to brotherly sympathy, can establish, at least in that one spot, the kingdom of heaven on earth.

Thus at the table of Judaism are seated the present and the past, with its beauty and its incongruousness—and the future, too, is within its ken. Some will say that the table is overcrowded, that we must oust those visitors of bygone times to make more room for new comers. No need for that, unless the past seeks to monopolise more than its fair share of space, and to crush out the present altogether. For we cannot break with our past. The past has left an indelible stamp on our character, on our very countenances, in the tones of our voices, in our occupations and our sympathies. Thus, whether we will or not, the past is always with us. "Each new man strikes root into a far fore-time." To some Jews reform and progress mean the snapping of the chain of tradition. To me progress means lengthening the chain, so as to make the present, too, a part of that tradition. Rabbinism, it is argued, must go, you must clear away the rubbish before you can rebuild. This attitude is a most unhappy one for progress itself. Rabbinism was a phase in the development of Judaism, the latter being almost inconceivable without the former. If we are to go forward—it is on the basis of the past, by seeking to understand the real meaning of the Jewish tradition, to get at its essence and not to repeat the conventional platitudes against it, which sound unnatural when coming from Jewish lips. To throw us back entirely upon the Bible, and to discard the labours of the Rabbis is a very great stride—backwards; it is to abandon that very right of individual judgment which the Rabbis exercised and we in our turn claim. So, by your leave, the old Rabbis shall yet remain as honoured guests at our table.

But, on the other hand, though we touch that which the past has hallowed, gently and reverently, yet may it be touched, where necessary, none the less firmly. Tradition is a chain of many links, some pure gold, others of inferior metal; if we remove the latter the chain will still hold so long as we weld the remaining links honestly, and add links of durable and genuine material. We need not always keep the high road that has become the way of common trade; we may fearlessly venture off into untrodden paths, and part company for a while with our guides. Perchance after crossing our Red Sea we may lose ourselves in some desolate wilderness and perish—then so much the worse for us, and so much the better for those who profit by our awful example. Yet this fate can hardly be ours if we use the teachings of the past to direct us in what we think necessary strayings from the beaten track of history.

The blue vault of heaven is the temple of Judaism, and its walls are ample enough to hold us all; and this feast of freedom must not find us the slaves of religious convention. For the door must be opened wide to give free entrance to all who would join the assembly. Let zealots beware lest the man who seeks to come in finds the door shut in his face. Ah! how she, to whom my text referred, regretted such an act. Her beloved knocked and she would not open, but soon she altered her mind and went to the door to call for him—too late, for he was gone. So it might happen that if Jews shut the door now, the wayfarer will pass from us to seek his entertainment elsewhere.

This is the Elijah for whom we still may hope, for the man who will "turn the heart of the fathers to the children and the heart of the children to their fathers"[1]—to reconcile, if it may be, the old with the new. And may we each, in his or her way, aid in this, the crying need of Judaism to-day; that the mission of Israel may fulfil itself, not in discord—or if discord is inevitable for the time—in the final concord that shall last for ever round the table of the Most High.

---

[1] Malachi iv. 6.

"A NEW SONG."

"Sing unto the Lord a new song."

THOUGH in sermons one need not give chapter and verse for all one's statements, yet it is usual to give a reference for the text. On the present occasion I omit to do so. For the words that I have quoted occur in effect in at least five places in the Psalter. The desire to sing unto the Lord a new song was thus shared by various poets. The longing after newness is no new thing: let us hope that it will never become an old thing. For if there is one thing certain, it is that unless new circumstances bring new inspiration, religion cannot be an actual force in men's lives. It was God Himself, who, in the 40th Psalm, put the new song into the Poet's mouth :—

"I waited patiently for the Lord; and He

inclined unto me, and heard my cry. He drew me up out of the pit of destruction, out of the mire of the swamp, and set my feet on a rock, and made firm my steps. And He put a new song into my mouth, of Praise unto our God: many see it, and fear, and trust in the Lord."

Now, if you look carefully into the Psalms in which the poet seeks a new song, and by God's aid finds it, you will notice very little novelty of expression. Like so many new and original products of the modern stage, these Psalms are old in form, and are not new in theme. The 98th Psalm, which calls upon Israel to sing a new song to God, is almost entirely composed of reminiscences from the Second Isaiah. Thus the novelty must be sought elsewhere than in mere originality of idea. It was the Second Isaiah who gave fullest voice to a great and glowing theory of Israel's mission—to the only true theory, or rather to the only theory that deserves to be true—that God is the God of Israel, and yet all men's God, that Israel was chosen to be

God's servant to carry light to the Gentiles; out of its own sufferings and trials to rise to a purer faith, to a more sturdy confidence in the righteousness of God, and to bring the whole world to recognise the morality and the goodness that rule men's affairs, and must be reflected in their lives. Now this view of Israel's mission was new and not old, and many ardent Jewish souls were attracted by the new message of Isaiah, who was even more poet than prophet. There arose a band of Psalmists who were touched by his divine fire, shared his Messianic hopes, dreamt with him of a great moral re-birth of mankind—a band of Psalmists who took up Isaiah's message and spread it on the wings of song. This great doctrine of the mission of Israel, of the Divine Judgment, of the presence of God in each human heart, and in the heart of humanity, is nowhere more adequately enunciated than in the Psalms in which the world is bidden to sing a new song to the Lord. They are all Messianic, all universal in tendency, all marked by a wondrous intensity, and by an equally wondrous liberality.

They show how possible it is for religious emotion to run broad and deep at one and the same time.

But again we are brought back to the question. If the Psalmists were merely echoing Isaiah's new doctrines, wherein lies the novelty of their own poems? It is true that when the Psalmist says: "Sing a new song to the Lord," the new song is not primarily the song he is singing, but the song that the peoples are one day to sing. But if there were nothing of novelty in this call for a new song, why should the poet harp so on the string that his songs are new? Novelty in fact there is, and very striking novelty. The Second Isaiah was a poet, who dreamt noble dreams for his people. But the Psalmists, who were among his immediate or later disciples, did more than this. They did not speak Isaiah's words, they put them into the people's mouth; not they, but the people spoke, or rather they led the song, and their people joined in the chorus. For these particular Psalms, in which animate and inanimate nature are bidden to sing a new song, were all written for public worship. Psalm xxxiii. is clearly congregational, so are xcvi., xcviii., and cxlix. Their hymnic character is so self-evident that most of them have been included in the service of the Synagogue up to this day, while Psalm xcviii. has been also incorporated into the daily service of the English Church since the year 1552. This was the novelty, to bring the great truths that Isaiah taught into the daily ritual, to use the noblest and most elevated doctrine as part of the liturgy, to transfer Isaiah's sentiments from the market-place to the house of God. And this is the lesson of all religious progress. The few originate, but the many are needed to make the new thing productive; the few think new thoughts, the many must find new forms in which to express them. The formulation of the highest truth needs constant revision, and even more surely do the forms in which that truth is clothed. When dogma takes the place of love, religion is dead. And a liturgy that cannot expand, that cannot absorb the best religious teaching of the age, that cannot dare to sing unto the Lord new songs, such a liturgy is a printed page, it is not a prayer fresh from the suppliant's heart.

So far, then, we have seen that there were times when Judaism was capable of accepting new truth, and of singing new songs to God based on that new truth. Judaism could adopt a wider hope, a fuller theory of God's relation to the world, and yet could do this without abandoning those essential elements which made it a special and historical religion. It could compose and sing new songs, or rather it could rewrite the old, could utilise current and well-worn phrases, and bring them into accord with more recent facts of religious experience. Now, as far as our own present and near future is concerned, we can anticipate no new religious truth of startling import; the great truths which we shall know have been already revealed. But I hope that it is not true that the new songs too have been already written. Tradition cannot thus be broken off in the very midst of its growth, for tradition in the Synagogue always meant the new on the basis of the old. The Jewish liturgy is full of undeveloped germs, and in many a neglected corner of it lie unperceived seeds of coming beauty, which will only be ripened by the rain and the sunshine of many ages, by forms of happiness and tribulation unknown to our fathers. Our better knowledge of the history of the origin of Judaism confirms this. At one time it was believed that all the Psalms were written by David, and that then inspiration ceased; we now know that nearly all the Psalms are of much later date than the Davidic age. We know that each fresh crisis in our national history gave birth to new songs; that the Babylonian exile and the epoch of the Return were rich in their poets and singers. So, too, the Maccabean revolt, with its religious and political rejuvenescence, produced numberless Psalmists, some of whom may have composed one or two of those very new songs which have provided our text to-day. After the Biblical canon was closed psalms were still written; for the strange collection of prayers, termed the Psalms of Solomon, prove that the power of psalmody was not yet extinct in the age of Pompey. The Apocryphal literature contains several psalms, and the compilers of the Synagogue liturgy shared the old Jewish genius for prayer-writing. At that time Jews were not content to praise God with their fathers' lips. Then came the *Poetanim*, the mediæval poetasters who wrote hymns and songs for the Synagogue, many of which have now been discarded by Orthodoxy itself. One cannot regret their loss, for though these piyutim or hymns were instinct with religious force, and strong with fervent faith, yet the cold and mechanical form in which they were cast froze out of them the undoubted emotional fire of their authors. Still these latter tried for a great aim; they sought to sing new songs of sorrow as fresh causes for lament arose in the Crusading ages; they sought to give voice to their feelings of joy as new proofs of the Divine providence were witnessed. There was no lyrical stagnation in a period that could add the *Adon Olam* as a permanent gem to our golden treasury of sacred song. And then came the decay. Judaism fell into its stereotyped stage; everything became rigid; the laws and the liturgy were codified, and men's emotions were reduced to a series of set tunes. The songsters ceased, and no new voices have been heard for more than three centuries.

But why should the process have stayed? Why are no new songs now written for the service of God? Have the Jews of to-day no new calls for praise and weeping? The past history of Israel could show no incident more world-moving, more unexpected, more providential, than the civil and political emancipation of the Jews in the present century. Where then were the new songs of thanksgiving that should have burst forth in a joyous flood from hearts overflowing with thankfulness? Here and there a solitary voice was heard, but there was silence in the camp—no new shouts of praise, no new songs of gladness. And again, when the pointed arrow of Russian persecution pierced millions of Jews with an edge more biting than the sword of mediæval fanaticism, where were the elegies, the tearful laments, the new songs, doleful as the doleful theme? A similar impotence marks our moments of less exceptional emotion than these. The blight of Puritanism has fallen on us. The Puritans wrought a great delivery in England, they freed men in body and soul, they were fervent, faithful servants of God, yet they failed to sweeten their deliverance by poetry, they sang no new songs to the Lord, and they made the very deliverance they wrought ugly and repellent. Righteousness is the root and the stem of the tree of life, but song and psalm are its leaf and its blossom.

We know in part why these new songs have failed us. In the first place, the Psalms are so full of spiritual good, their note is so various, they respond to so many of our moods, that the songs that were new in the Psalmist's days have never grown old in ours. Yet owing to this very popularity of the Psalms, their wide-spread use in every religious service of the civilised world, they have acquired a fixity in our services, they have become part and parcel of a stereotyped ritual, and have thus lost something of their spontaneity. One almost longs for less inspired songs, provided that they be new. One seeks variety and not sameness in one's prayers just as there is variety and not sameness in one's feelings. Does one feel alike every week? Yet one must pray alike every week. Oh for the old fluidity when the Poetan extemporised, for if his song was wanting in delicacy of form, it came fresh from his heart.

The unquestioned supremacy of the Psalms is thus the first cause of the dearth of new Jewish prayers. Next comes the difficulty of the language. Was it not partly from this difficulty that the successors of Mendelssohn failed to enrich the liturgy as the followers of Judas the Maccabee did? Was it not that the Maccabees prayed and sang in the language in which they thought, while we think in one language and pray in another?

Some people expect great things from the growing popularity of prayers in the vernacular, and no one can doubt that the introduction into the Synagogue of Bible readings in English has already had a marked effect for good in this country. The Chief Rabbi has himself adapted a beautiful English prayer, and it may be that when we can decide how far, and under what restrictions, English is to find a place in the liturgy, the new songs will not be wanting. Yet I cannot restrain the remark that what we need at present are a few simple, stirring Hebrew hymns, in which the thoughts should be new, but the language old; the ideas elevated, but the style such as a child could understand. There have been many modern writers of good Hebrew, but they have lacked the directness and the simplicity which are essential to hymns.

Lastly, and chiefly, in explaining the stoppage in the flow of poetical inspiration, we must not forget that the decay is only about as old as the invention of printing. What are three or four centuries in the thousands of years over which the history of Judaism extends? They are only a bad quarter of an hour which will pass away and be forgotten. A certain spiritual torpor, or rather, spiritual timidity, seized us in the sixteenth century. The old beliefs of Judaism were dearly cherished, and it seemed as if the only way to save them was by stunting them and preventing them from changing. Perhaps those that thought thus were right. But now Judaism has come into contact with a wider world, and yet Judaism is firmer and faster than ever. Our grasp on the great principles of our faith is, I think, surer than it ever was in the past, for we are becoming more confident of the future. We have a new, a wider hope, and our Judaism, becoming less doubtful of its power to rise, will essay again mighty flights into unknown realms of religious Psalmody.

Yet, even now, before Isaiah's dream realises itself in the coming ages, even now in our own little and prosaic lives, we must sing unto the Lord new songs. Every day that is added to the life of the Israelite race is a new miracle; every triumph of right over wrong, of truth over falsehood; every new victory of reason, every fresh discovery in science; every motive that restates the old belief in God's providence and Israel's mission; every hour of joy, every moment of suffering, is a provocation to all men for a new song. And the happy thing is that these new songs we can write and sing without being poets or musicians at all—by being simple, truthful men and women, touched by no higher talent than sincerity. An erroneous yet quaint translation of a Psalmic phrase tells us that "Unto God silence too is praise." The silent heart wells forth in melody sometimes more sweet than the sweetest of new songs. For every one knows the plague of his own heart, every one knows his own temptations, his own personal causes for gratitude and praise; and every heart can sing, to its own tune and in the language it alone understands, its own new songs to the Lord.

---

[1] Ps. lxv. 2.

THE LOVE OF MAN.

"*Thou shalt love thy neighbour as thyself.*" [1]

IF, my dear friends, we were really to love our neighbours as ourselves, we should love our neighbour with no little intensity. Yet, after all, we are told, Love thy neighbour as thyself; and the first implication is that one not only does naturally love oneself, but that one is even morally bound to do so. Now, in a sense, it is quite unnecessary to preach the doctrine of self-love. There are what Sir Thomas Browne would call " self-ended souls," whose whole life's sphere is bounded on every side by self; stay-at-home people, for whom there is no outside

---

[1] Levit. xix. 18.

world, or rather for whom the outside world exists as a frame to set off their own admirable picture. On the other hand, one cannot help seeing that this very selfishness may end in producing the opposite defect. In ages of materialism, a pessimistic view of life is rather more than less likely to prevail. Concentrated all in self, life loses for many interest and worth. If you are always looking at one portrait, though a master-artist drew it, the features will pall on you, and in the end its familiar lines become positively hateful. In this way the most selfish people often detest themselves; and hatred of others, because I find myself hateful, is a vice not restricted to philosophers.

Therefore, you see, it is not unnecessary to tell some people to love themselves, for by those words I mean: Make yourselves lovable, create a self that you may rightly dare to love. Are there not whole tracts of the microcosm which each of us is, left quite uncultivated? Are our everyday hunger and thirst, our desires for ease, our passionate longing to lead the fashion, our true selves? Selfishness such as this is mean and hateful, but not so the selfishness that might make of each of us a true human soul, in which mind and heart would produce flowers of light and loveliness. Love thyself, if thyself be a true self, the love of which cannot be selfish.

For the blossom of this perfect self-love is what we commonly call unselfishness, but might better be described as sympathy. "Love thy neighbour as thyself" is the ethical expression to this side of the perfected character. But I shall be asked: If a perfect character is producible by fully loving your own self—if your self be lovable, and you make it lovable— why should the maxim assume the form, Love thy neighbour? Because personal perfection is impersonal. What a poor and low idea of the perfectibility of the human soul must be held by one who can think that his perfection *can* be purely personal. Why, the ethical idea of God's own perfection is interpreted by His attribute of making others than Himself perfect. He cannot be loveworthy who does not wish others to be lovable; he is no true man who does not believe that others can be made lovable by his very love of them. The maxim, "Love thy neighbour as thyself," has thus an *actuality* which no sarcasm can minimise, for the practice of it proves its veracity, and helps to reconcile human nature to itself.

Yet it may be doubted whether any other saying has been productive of more unneighbourly bickering than the saying, "Love thy neighbour as thyself." Christianity claims it for its own, and Dr. Güdemann gravely tells us how astonished a recent Austrian Minister of Education was even to hear that the words occurred in the Old Testament. This is uncommon ignorance, let us hope; but it is usually said that the Old Testament bids Hebrew to love Hebrew, that the neighbour referred to as deserving love must be a member of the same religion. For the moment, let us suppose it to be so, for whatever else the maxim implies, it certainly does imply that much. My friends, if a modern Jewish version of Leviticus were produced, the compiler would indeed be impelled to bid Jew to love Jew. Little does the outside public know how unfounded is its charge of Jewish clannishness. Just as the ordinary Christian thinks that every Jew knows the Talmud by heart, so he thinks that every Jew loves every other Jew with a love that is the heritage of centuries of fellow-suffering. What a delusion! Jews love nothing so little as they do other Jews. Who say the worst things of Jews? Other Jews. Who have been the cause of the worst evils the Jews have suffered? Jews again.

When Eisenmenger had written his venomous attack on Judaism, which like a seed covered up in congenial soil, attracted little attention in his own time, but supplied when grown to maturity poisoned weapons to our foes—when this slander was written, who agitated for its publication? Former Jews. And worst of all, do any people profess a lower opinion of the Jewish character than the Jews themselves?—a character which, despite its blemishes, possesses the germs and some of the fruits of moral beauty. Love thy neighbour as thyself. Think well of your religion and of your race by understanding your religion and reading the records of your race's history. See what these Jews, whom we so loftily despise, have done, and what we other Jews might be doing, and take shame to ourselves that we love not our brethren more. Shame that we do so much by word and deed—chiefly by word—to make the name of Jew sound ill and ugly; that we call the altar of the Lord contemptible, in that we slander its priests, who should be ourselves. If a Jew is charged with meanness and overreaching, with cunning effort at dishonest gain, how his loving Jewish friends shrug their shoulders and say, "How like a Jew; we don't like to have anything to do with Jews," despising others with the contempt they themselves deserve. I do not counsel a Chauvinistic love-a-Jew-at-any-price policy, but a little blindness to a Jewish neighbour's faults, and a good deal more open-eyedness to a Jewish neighbour's virtues. Mutual respect is indeed one of the bases of social virtues. "For thus said the Holy One, blessed be He: My beloved children, do I lack anything which you could give me? I need nothing from you but that you should love one another, and respect each other, and that no sin or ugly thing be found in your midst."[1]

But we are always being told that the world is not so very large, and that all men are thus more or less neighbours. Neighbourly love must not be restricted to any one sect or section of neighbours. Yet we are often told that the blot on Judaism was that it did not quite reach this point, that it stopped short of it, though well within sight of it. If it be merely maintained that the complete doctrine of universal love is not clearly expressed in any one Pentateuchal sentence, I should admit the truth of the statement. It may even be fairly, though I think erroneously, contended that the Old Testament, in bidding men to love their neighbours, only implied that Israelite was to love Israelite. But two points must be carefully noted. The first is, that in the Old Testament the law of love is elsewhere amplified, as when we are persistently,

---

[1] *Tana d. b. E. R.*, ch. xxviii.

and even with pathetic pleading, bidden to love the stranger. Secondly, in the progress to which, within certain narrow limits, all ethical ideas are subject, the law of neighbourly love came early, and before the dawn of Christianity, to be interpreted in the widest and most general sense, by Jewish teachers. The doctrine of Hillel that this universal love is the fundamental principle of the Jewish law can be traced step by step from its formulation by Hillel in the period preceding the birth of Christianity, until its final and complete enunciation in the school of Rabbi Akiba, in the second century of the Christian era. In the Mishnah, Hillel's ideal Jew is "one who loves mankind." He does not say "who loves his enemies," partly because to say so is to talk paradox, but chiefly because his own loving and simple heart found no such a distinction as that between friend and foe. So his single rule was " Love all men."

In point of fact this universal love is justified by Jewish teachers on the ground of the unity of human nature itself. For note this striking contrast, pointed out by Dr. Güdemann.[1] In St. Matthew this love is based on the just remark that sun and rain alike come to the evil and the good. That is to say, while the Gospel confirms universal love by appealing to the unity of external nature, Judaism confirms it by appealing to the unity of human nature. Ben Azai goes no further than "this is the Book of the generations of man," from which words of Genesis he infers that the very fact of common humanity is a sufficient reason for a man to love his kind. "Beloved is man," says Rabbi Akiba, "for he was created in the image of God." This is the keynote of developed Judaism. Man in his entirety is beloved of God, and must therefore be beloved of man. In this doctrine lies the hope at once of personal and of general regeneration, in the belief that human nature is one, and lovable, and perfectible, that the heart of man is not the devil's playground, that it is on human nature and its possibilities that the progress of the world relies.

---

[1] *Nächstensliebe* (Vienna, 1890).

A modern mystic with whom all religious minds have something in common, Swedenborg, fell prostrate before this great doctrine when he exclaimed, "My reward for loving my neighbour as myself will be that I shall come to love him more than myself." He, too, felt that man is capable of this love that transcends and yet recognises self. While Judaism keeps its hold on this view it has a living social mission, to preach love for a loveworthy self, love for brethren in faith and blood, love for mankind—lovable because of its manhood. What a responsibility is thus cast upon each of us to find this ideal of a true manly life and to fix that ideal in practice; so to live that we "be not merely lightly dipped but deeply grained" in generous, honest humanity, that the Jew, hopeful for the future, may tell the world again, "Love thy neighbour as thyself," and show the world how to do it.

THE NEGATIVE FORM OF THE "GOLDEN RULE."

When I last occupied this pulpit I spoke on the text, "Thou shalt love thy neighbour as thyself." I tried to indicate some of the stages by which this maxim became the Golden Rule of conduct, until it acquired the widest influence in social morality by its adoption in the Gospels under a form which may be summarised as: Do as you would be done by. Now Hillel's death coincided almost exactly with the birth of Jesus, and I ask your attention to-day to the terms in which the Jewish Rabbi enunciated the fundamental sentiment which has become associated with the name of Jesus—a sentiment, the acceptance of which renders the life of men possible in society with one another.

Hillel, on a famous occasion, said: "*What is hateful to thyself, do not to another.*"[1]

This version of the Golden Rule is, you will note, stated in negative terms. It does not bid men to do what they love; it bids them not to do to others what they would hate if done to themselves. Curiously enough, the negative form occurs again in an early Jewish work, viz., in the Book of Tobit, where the words of Hillel are almost identically repeated. Philo, too, the noble Jewish Alexandrian, spread the same doctrine in the same negative terms among his Hellenistic friends. But here is, I think, an interesting fact. The negative form of the Golden Rule not only preceded Christianity, it also survived it. The negative form is quoted by certain early Christian authorities as identical in force and meaning with the positive maxim. So St. Paul, in his Epistle to the Romans, explaining that the Decalogue, forbidding various unsocial acts, might be summed up in the Old Testament saying, "Thou shalt

---

[1] Talmud, *Sabbath*, p. 31a.

love thy neighbour as thyself"—St. Paul, I say, justifies this attempted summarisation by the remark, "Love worketh no ill to his neighbour, therefore love is the fulfilling of the law,"[1] clearly giving the love its negative application, making it signify the complete avoidance of what is harmful rather than the performance of what is helpful.

I do not know when it began to be urged that the negative form of the Golden Rule was lacking in completeness; I think it must have been when it became tolerably certain that Hillel's saying anticipated the Gospel by about half a century. To reproach Hillel, however, for an incomplete sense of social duties is peculiarly inapt. For the same Hillel, who used the words of our text, also said, in an even more famous utterance: "Be of the disciples of Aaron, loving peace and pursuing peace; *loving thy fellow-creatures,* and bringing them nigh to the Torah."[2] Thus Hillel taught in positive terms the duty of loving all men;

---

[1] Romans xiii. 10.   [2] Mishnah, *Aboth* i. 12.

but I fancy he had some sufficient motive for formulating the Golden Rule in negative terms. The negative form is, in fact, more fundamental, whether from the point of view of human reason or of human nature.

To see the matter in its true light, one must carefully consider the circumstances under which Hillel spoke. You remember how a heathen went to Shammai, and asked him to teach him the Law while he stood on one foot. Shammai did what most people would have done under similar provocation. He showed his questioner the door, and, being ungifted with Hillel's gentle tolerance, perhaps he stood on one foot while he did it. But when Hillel was accosted by the same impatient inquirer he did not get angry. A man once bet another four hundred coins that he would make Hillel lose his temper. He tried, but Hillel kept his temper, and the man lost his money. So, when the would-be proselyte asked Hillel to teach him the Law while he stood on one foot, Hillel calmly answered: "What to thyself is hateful, do not to another. This is the whole Law, the rest is but commentary." In the seventeenth century, Rabbi Samuel Edels, the renowned Talmudist, asked, "Why did not Hillel say to him, 'Thou shalt love thy neighbour as thyself'?" Because Hillel had to go straight to the root of the whole matter; he had to tell his questioner a truth on which the law of love is itself a commentary. He was not offering the perfected Law, but was giving the heathen, with his one-legged philosophy, another leg to stand on; he was offering to him the principle without which there would be no sure foundation for social intercourse. If Hillel had said, "Love thy neighbour," or "Do to him as you would have him do to you," the heathen might have replied, "That is all very well, but I do not want anything from my neighbour; I want neither his love nor his favours. Why, then, should I love him or do him service?" And I think the objection would have needed more argument for its refutation than a man on one foot would have listened to with patience. Besides, Hillel would have been compelled to fall back on:

"What is hateful to yourself, do not to another," as the justification of the law of love. Hence he stated at the outset the axiom itself, and the proselyte saw at a glance that here was the fundamental basis of social and religious virtue. I may not need my neighbour's love, but I cannot live with him if he hate me. The negative form seems to me to go deeper to the heart of the problem.

This will be quite evident if I contrast very briefly the two opposing theories of human rights which now prevail; the socialistic view and its antithesis, the individualistic view. Mr. Herbert Spencer, the champion of individualism, has recently published a book entitled "Justice," which was, I fear, obsolete before it was written. Mr. Spencer, with most philosophical inaccuracy, repeats the baseless statement that the social ethics of the Old Testament are altogether negative and not positive. The principle of justice, he thinks, may be enunciated thus: "Every man is free to do that which he wills, provided he infringes not the equal freedom of any other man." Mr. Spencer may call this positive if he likes, but so far as it is true, what is it but Hillel's maxim formulated in more modern language? What is Mr. Spencer's criterion of freedom? The non-interference with me by others. What, again, is Mr. Spencer's condition of freedom? The non-interference by me with others. This does not seem very different from Hillel's more terse utterance: "What is hateful to you, do not to others." Mr. Spencer's principle is thus in essence as negative as can be. On the other hand, poles asunder from Mr. Spencer's individualistic theories stands the socialistic view. It differs, however, from individualism not so much in its ends as in its means. Sensible socialism, scientific socialism, does not demand an equal distribution of property, does not claim an equal reward for unequal services. What socialism demands of the State and of Society, nay, what it has the right to demand, is that neither the State nor Society shall by unjust artifices keep down one man and elevate another; it demands not that all shall draw equal prizes, but that all shall have equal chances. Socialism, in this sense, bases itself on the principle that man, by his manhood, has an inalienable right to the free exercise of his powers, to the unimpeded use of his abilities, and to the peaceful enjoyment of the fruits of his labours. In other words, socialism and individualism, in so far as they are true schemes of moral conduct, are based on a principle that comes very much to the same maxim as that on which Hillel thought the law was founded.

Now let us look at the matter from another side. Has it ever struck you how large a part of popular wisdom is cast in a negative from; how many proverbs, whether in etiquette or ethics, begin with *Do not?* Of the Ten Commandments, seven are negative. In the Old Testament there are, according to the traditional Jewish enumeration, 248 affirmative commandments, supposed to equal the number of our limbs; while there are 365 negative precepts, one for every day in the year. This is unhappily a true proportion between good and evil: you need to exert all your powers, use all your limbs, to do good; while to do evil, you need but let the days roll on, and the opportunities for harm come of their own accord. Think what the world would be if men, though they did no good, yet did no wrong. The world would be an earthly paradise. No falsehood, no violence, no revenge, no dishonesty, no arrogance, no jealousy, no war! No barriers to intellectual and moral progress! Was not Hillel, my friends, a wise man? "What is hateful to thyself, do not to another." When we remember how great is our power for evil, how small our power for good; how, in the words of the doctor-philosopher, "we are beholden to every man we meet that he doth not kill us"; how

> The evil that men do lives after them,
> The good is oft interred with their bones;

how

> Men's evil manners live in brass, their virtues
> We write in water,

—when we remember all this, we must sadly admit that though Hillel's maxim may be enunciated while we stand on one foot, we must take a firm grip of earth with both our feet if we would even try to obey it.

The demand made on man not to injure his fellow-man is then the Jewish form of the Golden Rule. Alas that Jewish history should have been fated to supply so full a commentary on it. For how many centuries has Judaism been appealing to the world to obey this rule of conduct? The Jew did not dare to ask: Give me your friendly hand to raise me; he meekly pleaded: Lay not your unfriendly hand so heavily on me to crush me down. He feared to ask: Love me! He asked: Do not hate me. He asked for non-interference, to be permitted to live. I do not expect, the Jew said in effect, I do not expect to be placed in your palaces; but at least leave the gate of my Ghetto open. Did you ever hear to-day of Russian Jews demanding rights and privileges, powers and favours, from the Czar's Government? Nay; they cry, Leave us alone and let us breathe. How can God's highest truth direct a world which has not yet fully learned the simplest fundamental rule of moral equity?

Happily for men's future hopes, O Hillel, thou friend of peace, thou lover of thy fellow-men, there are many of our own and of other faiths who obey thy plain guiding rule, who not hating others may become like thee, lovers of their kind!

The gratitude of the world, and of Judaism with it, is due to the Gospels for popularising, in theory at least, the Golden Rule of conduct. The Golden Rule of the Gospels is a useful working compromise, but while it is not the fundamental statement of the law of love, neither is it the fullest or highest statement of that law. It bids man do as he would be done by. But loving is something more than *doing*. One must do lovingly, but one must also think lovingly of others, and feel lovingly for them, ay—and this is the widest stretch of of love—one must weep for them when one can do nothing to soften their pain, when one can only stand by them, look on, and love them.

"What is hateful to thyself, do not to another." From this the ascent is inevitable to the higher truth, "Love thy neighbour as thyself." Nay, more. Love is the one touch of divine nature that makes all men akin. And man, starting from the basis of non-hatred of his fellow-man, will soon reach the stage of loving him. Yet he will not rest even there, he will pass onward to realise all that his nature is capable of. From this love of his fellow he will pass to the love that makes a man of him, and his heart will be warm with the love of God. The last word of social ethics is, "Thou shalt love thy neighbour as thyself;" but the last word of religion is, "Thou shalt love the Lord thy God."

THE LOVE OF GOD.

" Grace and truth shall meet one another,
Righteousness and peace shall kiss;
Truth shall spring out of the earth,
Righteousness look down from heaven." [1]

TRUTH in itself is a worthy end, but no truth is fruitful unless it be also lovable. How to make truth lovable, that is the problem of religion. Judaism has solved it rather well by hallowing and beautifying knowledge. Herein lies the virtue of a religion which is in a sense a learned religion, it sanctifies the exercise of the intellect, it glorifies truth, and sets a garland of loveliness on her brow. It feels that grace by itself is not enough, nor is truth alone sufficing.

---

[1] Psalm lxxxv. 11, 12.

But when grace and truth meet, when righteousness and peace kiss one another, when truth shall spring out of the earth, righteousness look down from heaven, you have the picture of an ideal world. Man and God join strength, and truth becomes fruitful, because it becomes lovable.

Let me show you that this thought has a practical importance. We Jews, who rather pride ourselves in having an undogmatic religion, are in some danger of treating our Judaism as though it were dogma and nothing else. If I were to ask you what Judaism is, I fear that you would tell me that while it insists on righteousness and a moral life as other religions do, Judaism specifically teaches the dogma of the Unity of God. We are almost inclined to make a fetish of the Unity of God; we are supposed to repeat the declaration of the Unity three times a day; we lisp it as infants, we proclaim it as men, we whisper it dying. Now the Unity of God is an essential and fundamental truth; but a religion does not exist, does not deserve to exist, merely to teach a truth, however important. Does the Unity of God inspire us to lead moral lives, does it offer a solace for the ills of existence, does it make our human souls one with the God's whose Unity is on our lips? Yes, it can do all this. For the one God whose Unity we proclaim is the God whom we must love. Our truth becomes fruitful because it is associated with love.

It is no accident that the duty of loving God is so frequently tacked on to the declaration of His Unity in the Book of Deuteronomy. "Hear, O Israel, the Lord our God, the Lord is one. And thou shalt love the Lord thy God." I say that this connection is not casual, it is a necessary connection. Unity is strength in love. You do not really love a dozen people whole-heartedly at once. And especially the pure, unsensuous idea of loving God seems impossible except to those who thoroughly and in an unqualified manner accept the Unity of God and His incorporeality. It is no accident again that the Synoptic gospels only once refer to this idea of loving

God beyond quoting the passage just given from Deuteronomy. At all events, despite the fine use made of the doctrine of Love by St. John, it was Judaism which more fully absorbed this idea of the love of God into its every-day liturgy. At times Jews were called upon to die to proclaim God's Unity before the world, but they lived and spiritually thrived, nay, they gained the very power to die for the Unity, because they loved the truth which they maintained. Their strength was not wrested from obstinacy; it was given by love. It has been attempted, I know, to deny this. Dr. Georg Winter, in an oft-quoted essay on "the love of God in the Old Testament" (Stade's *Zeitschrift*, 1889, pp. 211-246), suggests that in Deuteronomy the love of God has only a ritual sense, that its very connection with the doctrine of the Unity implies that to love God means to worship Him exclusively, to obey His law, and to acknowledge no other God beside Him. Dr. Winter further contends that the love of God only attained an extra-ritualistic significance when Judaism was superseded. But this theory does violence to the facts. Can any one recall the many glowing words of Deuteronomy as a whole without feeling that the love of God is there something more than a mere worship—than a mere proclamation of His uniqueness? At all events the love of God became very early the leading principle of Judaism. The school of Rabbi Akiba (Talm. Jer. *Berach.* I.) took the whole Shema'—not the first verse only—as the fundamental document of Judaism.[1] Every religion sooner or later tries to formulate itself, to put itself into a few simple rules. This tendency is seen in the teaching of Jesus, but before him already in the Old Testament, and in the words of his nearer predecessors like Hillel, the love of the one God, with its corollary the love of man, became the simplest and ultimate epitome of Judaism.

How, amid all the cumbersome legalistic expansions of the Law, these principles became more and more the basis of Judaism, how they were sifted and brought ever closer

---

[1] The Shema' consists of Deuteronomy vi. 4-9.

into accord with the facts of human experience, the Jewish ethical literature shows. It is a grave misfortune that our ethical books are written in a language that so few Jews can read. If it be true that men hold *omne ignotum pro magnifico*, how magnificent should Judaism seem to most Jews. You little dream what you lose by neglecting your ethical and religious literature. I am not thinking so much of the Talmud or of the Midrashim. I am thinking rather of the works of men who helped Judaism forward in times nearer ours, who put the old imperfect truths into language, still imperfect, but ever growing truer. Have you ever heard of the "Rokeach," a book splendid, yet simple in mystic devoutness, written by Eleazar of Worms in the thirteenth century? Have any of you tried to read that ascetic yet God-inspired and God-inspiring treatise of Bechai, called "The Duties of the Heart"—a title which is in itself an inspiration? Nay, how many of you ever read the noble introduction of Maimonides to his work, "The Strong Hand"? Would it be impossible for you Jewish students[1] to found here a modest ethical society to read your own Jewish ethical books? Read them, and the charm of them will seize you, they will help you to love Judaism and to love God with a love all the sweeter because it would come to you after labour.

Now I have mentioned these books not to introduce a digression, but to give point to the remark that the love of God is the beginning and the end of Judaism. While in Bechai's "Duties of the Heart" the love of God is the final goal, in Maimonides' "Strong Hand," and in Eleazar's "Rokeach," the love of God is the starting-point. And what is this love of God, what does it mean, what does it demand of us, what does it offer in return? Ah! there must be no bargaining here. Spinoza said, "You must not tell God, I will love you if you love me." In the Bible, and occasionally in our liturgy, man's love to God is based

---

[1] This sermon was preached in the Cambridge Synagogue.

naturally enough on gratitude, on God's love to man. But this is just what I mean when I say that Judaism has developed, for Jewish tradition in its highest exponents got beyond this stage. In the Jewish prayer אהבה רבה,[1] a prayer unique in the world's liturgies, the love of God to man and of man to God are put beautifully side by side without a suspicion of there being a *quid pro quo*. And so in the Midrash[2] a Rabbi says: "Though God torment me and embitter my life, still shall He dwell in my heart." And as our love of God does not grow out of gratitude, so the result of our love of God is not adulation. God wants imitation, not flattery. Our love of God must make us imitate Him, must lead us to that *Imitatio Dei* which is the favourite and the fond ideal of the oldest teachers of post-Biblical Judaism.

There are two opposite trains of thought in the Rabbinical literature. On the one hand,

---

[1] *Authorised Daily Prayer Book*, p. 39.
[2] *Cantic. Rabb.*, I. 13.

God is not like man, His qualities are incomparable to ours; on the other hand, God is actually compared to man in several passages, and the very habit of bringing out men's faults by contrasting them with God's excellences implies that the Rabbis felt the faults and the excellences to be commensurable, to be one in kind, and that the faults might be merged in the excellences. The acme of the love of God is reached in this *Imitatio Dei*, for just when this love of God attains its highest spiritual elevation, then it becomes filled with moral content, with human as well as divine love. "Be like God," said Abba Saul,[1] "if you would honour Him; as He is merciful and gracious, so be thou merciful and gracious." Only notice this difference between the Jewish and other views of philanthropy. You must love man by loving God, not love God by loving man. "Love God and make Him lovable to others."[2] Surely this was the last and highest word of religion.

---

[1] *Sifre Deut.* vi. 5.   [2] *Mechilta*, Shira 3.

But you will again ask, what does Judaism mean by the love of God? The inward sign of the love of God cannot be put into any but mystical language. It is an influence on our lives that makes our living a godly living, it moves our heart till it beats in unison with God's, it is a great and irresistible longing, a תאוה גדולה, almost an ecstasy. But the outward signs of the love of God can be more simply described. He who loves God will be distinguished by an exquisite *gentleness*. "They who are abased but abase not others, who hear themselves reproached but make no retort, who act from love of God and rejoice in suffering, of them Scripture says:[1] 'They that love Him are like the sun when he goeth forth in his might.'"[2] A fine idea; like the sun they are gentle and strong, their flight is masterful, but there is healing in their wings.

And, because the lover of God is gentle and fearless, he will be gifted with an all-pervading *cheerfulness*. He does all things with joy. It

---

[1] Jud. v. 31.   [2] T. B. *Sabbath*, 88b.

he renounces the world, he will renounce it without despising it. The keynote of Judaism in the past was its inherent joyousness; its happiness because of its love. "I am so happy in my Judaism," said Frankl, the late Rabbi of Berlin. Are we happy in our Judaism? Hardly so; because, to use a fine phrase of Mr. Schechter's, we love God not with our own hearts, but with our fathers' hearts. We do this and that Jewish ceremony to please our fathers; we preserve this or that Jewish custom to keep in touch with our history, when we should do and preserve them to get into touch with God. And our loss is bitter indeed. We Jews are no longer optimists; we are becoming despondent with the rest, we are growing old and cheerless like the world. Oh, but you say, can I become cheerful at your bidding, can I do my work in joy, because you tell me to smile? To which I answer: Think of the daring of Deuteronomy which, though it does not include the love of God in the Ten Commandments, still sets forth in so many sharp, clear-cut words the order: "Thou *shalt* love the Lord thy God." Can I be ordered to love? I think so, and Judaism always thought so. Habit makes character; that is the philosophy of Judaism in a sentence. The olden Jew learned to love God in every act of his life; his love made every act a joy to him. This, I admit, was a very difficult ideal to maintain in practice. Hard it is to live the conventional parts of our lives in cheerful love of God. But it is not so hard to learn to love Him with our best, in our highest moments, if not at all times, in our intellectual pursuits, in our direct action on the thoughts and lives of others. And if you can train your hearts to love Him, be sure that your lips will be wreathed in smiles. Though the world frown on you you will not grieve; though God hide His face from you, though you fail, still you will love Him; though hope deferred make you aweary, you still will say: "I sleep, but my heart waketh."

When this joyous glow plays round a gentle heart the product is the final mark of the love of God, viz., *Enthusiasm*. Enthusiasm is the glorification of the end aimed at, the gentle oblivion of one's own individual service in the end attained, the cheerful disregard of failure, equanimity in success. In a word, enthusiasm is the energising of love. He who lacks this enthusiasm is stopped by trifles because he fears he is seeking trifles. He dreads to find his ideals disproportionate to the effort made to reach them; he thinks things small and petty because love has not touched them into greatness and worthiness. Do not be alarmed at enthusiasm: do not fear either the word or the thing; learn to feel. Especially as Jews we must learn again how to feel. We have kept our hearts too long in chains; let us free our hearts, let us give fair play to them.

And finally, let me repeat that while the love of God is based on reverence, on the fear of God, it casts out all other fear. Young Jews are told and need to be told: Do not be ashamed of your religion in public; profess your religion bravely in the open, attempt no cowardly concealment. This is a true and necessary counsel. But there is an opposite counsel which is true and even more imperative. Do not be ashamed of your Judaism in private, profess it bravely in the silence and isolation of your own rooms. We are all afraid of cant, and it is a healthy fear. But we carry the fear of cant with us when we are alone, alone with our own hearts. We fancy that to assume a virtue in private when we do not parade it in public is dishonest and unmanly. But this is not flying from cant, it is flying from candour. Often I have felt ashamed to pray to God in private because I could not say in public that I loved Him; because I would not pretend before others, I would forsooth pretend before myself! Well, let me ask you to avoid this pitfall. I tell you, do not be ashamed when you are alone. Let the world be a little deceived in you. Keep a little of yourselves for your own privacy, some of the blossoms, nay, the choicest flower, of your love of God, for God's own eyes. When you are alone, do not be ashamed to pray, do not be afraid to love God. It is easier to pray in public than in private: the courage is needed when you are alone. Love God bravely and you will find that courage; it will strengthen you to do, to suffer, and to live—gentle, cheerful and enthusiastic, because you love God.

THE HATRED OF EVIL.

"*O ye that love the Lord, hate evil.*"[1]

I HAVE so often derived comfort from an idea conveyed by the wording of this simple text, that I venture to call your attention to the exact terms of the phrase which I have just quoted, for in it lies a great hope and a mighty stimulus. "O ye that love the Lord, hate evil." Few indeed must be the lovers of the Lord if the sign and mark of them is their hatred of evil. But the psalmist appeals to those who already love the Lord, and implores them to hate evil; implying, let us dare hope,

---
[1] Ps. xcvii. 10.

that the love of God may be a *preliminary* to this hatred, that man may love God even as he is, a man with evil in his heart as well as good.

For think of this: our text bids us to hate evil, not to run away from it. Hatred implies relationship of some kind, quite as strongly as love does. You do not hate things or persons who are out of your lives, who never cross your path. How foolish then are they who attempt to place our evil instincts outside our real selves, who even deny that our lower nature belongs to God equally with our higher. This thought would depose God from His throne, and estrange the Father from His children's hearts. Is a father father indeed, when his children are thrust from him at the very moment when their weakness most needs his strength? Does a King rule, when his subjects pass most of their lives in open revolt against him? If God can be served only by good, only by our better selves, then the world is less than half His. For look around and see how hideously commonplace is vice and sin and crime. Look into your own hearts and see how mean and selfish and ungodly man made in God's image can be. Shall God be robbed of His divine right because we are so human?

"Ah, pessimist!" you retort, "this is the doctrine of despair." Nay, it is the doctrine of hope, and it seems to me a real doctrine of Judaism. Though Judaism feared to adopt consistently Isaiah's bold declaration that God Himself created evil,[1] and thus must use evil as part of His divine design; though Judaism, between God and the evil in man, has often interposed an evil spirit dependent on God, yet external to Him; still Judaism teaches that man will not serve God best by vilifying himself, by degrading, by misunderstanding himself. Just because our nature is an *organic* unity, compounded of two elements, therefore in reference to our duty to God, we dare not attempt a logical differentiation, but must use the evil that is in us as well as the good, to do God's work in the world. This thought involves the corollary that my evil heart is I, no less

---

[1] Isaiah xlv. 7.

than my good heart; and that if I would live as God wills me to live, I must utilise my passions, and must perfect my lower instincts to love God with them, so to serve Him that His sovereignty over me is not eclipsed by the sin of which I am capable or the sin which I do.

There is a passage in the Talmud which at first sight is so quaint that some of you may even smile when I recite it, but the explanation of it may, I hope, render my meaning clearer than I can set it in my own words. The passage is in Berachoth 5*a*, and the Biblical phrases it quotes all occur consecutively in the tenth verse of Psalm iv., which I had better read beforehand: "Be ye angry, and sin not: commune with your own heart upon your couch, and be still." The following is R. Levi ben Hama's comment on this verse: " Ever let a man excite his good inclination against his bad inclination, for it is said, 'Be ye angry, and sin not.' If he conquer it, good; if not, let him engage in the Torah, for it is written, 'Commune with your own heart.' If this conquers the evil inclination, good; if not, let him read the Shema,[1] as it is said, 'Upon your couch.' If this succeed, good; if not, let him remind the evil inclination of the day of death, as it is said, 'And be still.'"

Here we have a fourfold scheme for resisting the importunities of the evil element in human nature. First, to overthrow evil, we are bidden to be angry with it. There is no doubt that anger has been the common characteristic of all moral reformers. Professor Huxley has rightly eulogised the anger of the prophets, and even in our own century the angry men— like Carlyle and Ruskin—have left the deepest mark on their times. Anger, however, is essentially a signal that the moral equilibrium is disturbed, and thus itself needs redress. "Thrice Moses was angry," says the Midrash,[2] "and thrice the Law was hidden from him." Anger, indeed, is but the trumpet-blast to battle; it does not constitute the battle itself. R. Levi bids us engage in the Law as a further specific against temptation. We need all the good that

---

[1] Deut. vi. 4—9.   [2] *Leviticus Rabba,* ch. xiii.

our character is capable of to make our lives aught but caricatures of manliness. "Engage in the Torah" and thereby drive out evil. For what is our Law but a scheme of righteous living, a filling of our hearts and selves with God's inspiring presence? You remember, in the beautiful early morning prayer, how, after enumerating several social virtues and various forms of benevolence, the paragraph closes with the words, "But the study of the Law is equivalent to them all."[1] Indeed it is equivalent to them all, for a life according to the Torah includes these virtues, and more; it gives these virtues the added power to transcend mere virtuous doing, it makes the virtues sparks and gleams of God's light, before which evil must hide its darkened—and, in a literal sense, diminished—head. To study the Law, to fill our minds with true thoughts and with noble ideals, is a sure means of crowding out the false and the ignoble, and of diminishing the sum total of evil.

---

[1] *The Authorised Daily Prayer Book*, ed. Rev. S. Singer, p. 5.

Is this enough? Anger against sin, zeal in virtue—will these so perfect us that evil shall lose its power over us? Nay, it is not enough. Before we turn to R. Levi's third specific against evil, let us for a moment consider the fourth element of his advice. "Recall the day of death," he says, in the struggle against sin. This is true counsel, but imperfect. The anticipation of death and the fear of retribution do withhold most from serious sin, but it is clearly explicit sin that is thereby prevented rather than sin itself, a horror of the consequence, not detestation of the act; the fear of evil to come does not exorcise evil present, least of all does it destroy that wrong conception of the meaning of evil which constitutes its power. But R. Levi gives us another piece of advice, and this, to my thinking, is the pith of his plan, this has been to me the most solacing thought of all. If your anger and your virtues fail—if, I venture to add, the fear of final retribution fail—then says Rabbi Levi, "when evil accosts you, *read the Shema.*"

Is this bathos or what? Read the Shema to

evil and blunt its point? How? The Rabbi, you will note, conceives the scene shifted; it is now night, when evil comes to most men, most alluringly, most perilously strong. Read the Shema? Yea, read it: "And thou shalt love the Lord Thy God with *all* thy heart." There is a remark in an old Midrash [1] which asks, "In the Shema, where it is written, Thou shalt love the Lord thy God, why has the word for *heart* a double letter?" The question is trivial, the answer is an impressive truth. The double letter implies, says the Midrash, that "man must love God with his whole heart, with his evil inclination no less than with his good." What can the Midrash mean by this extraordinary paradox? In this plea for loving God with our evil impulses, can we not detect a sense that man's sinfulness is part of his power for good, that he can only become a complete man by using his lower passions as part of his divinest self? If we think of this, if we absorb this belief, how can sin be dangerous any longer? For we should feel that our

---

[1] Sifre to Deut. iv. 10.

passions, our evil impulses are God's, that we must use them, and not abuse them, that God accepts us as we are, frail, imperfect, and earthly, but that He says to us, "Being what you are, use your whole selves to love Me; use your evil to serve Me too: do not surrender to your lower nature, but do not vilify it, or abuse it; elevate it to Me, and use it as a handmaid to the higher." In practice we follow an opposite tack. We try to suppress evil in the young; with what success, in God's sacred name, I repeat, look around and see! The vilification of human nature has been a favourite device of the churches and the creeds, and science has echoed the cry, and bids us look how small, how mean, how vicious, how animal we are. The novelist who has just died, and has left a void in our imaginations, took up the parable; yet even he wrote of his Dr. Jekyll and Mr. Hyde as though man's good self and his evil self were separable forces. The Rabbi was a better philosopher. "Love the Lord thy God with all thy heart, with thy good and with thy evil inclinations."

May we not dare to teach the boy to use his passions aright, not merely to put them out of sight; enable him to become a complete man by cultivating all his impulses? At least, let us, as grown men, learn to love God so that our hearts shall be perfect with Him, that we refuse to soil our hands as little as our thoughts with dishonesty, or profane our bodies as little as our hearts with unchastity, but love Him in these ways too; and without repressing or stifling half ourselves, curb our vices by remembering that by the misuse of our passions and even of our lowest bodily functions we are offending against the law of our being. Such an attitude towards evil draws its fangs, and even makes of it a power for good. Passion becomes love, ambition becomes a desire for human approval and sympathy, greed for wealth may be hallowed and narrowed into an unselfish anxiety for those dear and near to us. "If it were not for the evil inclination," said a Rabbi, "no man would build a house or marry a wife";[1] a remark which brings home

---

[1] *Genesis Rabba*, § 10.

my point that evil has a part to play in our lives, and it is only we who give it the mastery by forgetting that it, too, comes from God, and is an instrument which we must convert to God's purpose.

One point more. Why did the mediæval Jews show so much tenderness to returned apostates? Why did they receive them back with a love almost womanly in its gentle forgetfulness of the past, in the renewed rapture of the present? Why did the Jewish sages, even earlier, say of the penitent wicked that he was *perfectly* righteous? This was not because they held sin a light thing, to be pardoned and forgotten as though good and evil were identical. But they perhaps fancied that a man who had seen sin face to face, had tasted of its sweets, had yielded to its embrace, had finally thrown himself free, and crippled and maimed had crept alive back to truth, that such a man was more of a man than before; that he was now nearer to the *realisation* of the evil in him, nearer to that true use of it which should make his righteousness henceforth perfect. My friends, not all of us can go through the fire and come out alive; for us is the prayer, "O God, lead us not into temptation."[1] But we need not fathom the depths of sin to understand that we have a duty to God with the sin of which we are capable, that, without any intermediate yielding, we may learn to hate evil with that perfect hatred which hates best because it knows itself to be an aspect of love. "Ye that love the Lord hate evil"—hate it that we may win our whole selves for God and good. "Let us be angry and sin not; let us commune with our own hearts on our couch, and be still": at peace with our selves if we are perfect and heart-whole with the Lord our God.

---

[1] *Authorised Daily Prayer Book*, p. 7.

PART II.

THE OMNIPRESENCE OF GOD.

"Whither shall I go from Thy spirit? or whither shall I flee from Thy face? If I climb up into heaven, Thou art there; or make Hades my bed, lo, Thou art there. If I lift up the wings of the dawn, and settle at the farther end of the sea, even there Thy hand shall lead me, and Thy right hand shall hold me."[1]

THE thought to which the Psalmist gives expression in these magnificent words has become a commonplace of modern theology. "Where is God?" asks the child, and we answer, half automatically, "God is everywhere." In the development of the Jewish religion this conception of God's omnipresence was only reached at a comparatively late period, and it was for long crossed and obscured

---

[1] Psalm cxxxix. 7-10 (Prof. Cheyne's translation).

by other simpler and more childish notions. To the moral attributes of Deity, to His supreme pity and justice, there are endless references in the Psalter and the Prophets; to the Divine omnipresence there are but few. And indeed there is an element of philosophy and of mysticism in this conception, to neither of which the native Hebrew mind was pre-eminently prone. "God is everywhere," we tell our children; but the words, I imagine, make but a small impression upon them, and they will more habitually picture God as a localised and limited personality like themselves, sitting, perchance, upon some high and lofty throne in the distant heavens, but with ears and eyes that can hear and see everything in all the universe around Him. Such a conception of God, human, anthropomorphic though it be, does not preclude the idea of God's wise and loving omniscience being fully realised as well, and therefore, for the stage of existence at which it is held, it is healthy and unobjectionable. And yet we say it is a childish conception, and we welcome allusions to the Divine omnipresence such as those in the 139th Psalm and in Solomon's prayer. We regard them as beautiful and true, answering to a need we dimly feel in our life-long struggle towards the understanding of God.

What lies, as it were, at the back of this dim feeling? Is there any value for religion in the doctrine that God, as we say to our children, is neither here nor there, but everywhere. What do we mean by it? It may be—indeed, I think it is—well worth while to make this dogma of the Divine omnipresence less abstract and less barren by attempting to fix its place in our total conception of God and of His relation to the universe and to man. And it may be that we shall find that this dogma has more connection with our religious life than at the first blush might, too lightly, have been supposed.

Now, first of all, those of us who desire to fashion such an idea of God as may not be hindered or harmed by that small modicum of science which we are now unable to avoid, even if we wished, will find in this doctrine of God's universality much comfort and support. It has become increasingly difficult for any grown man or woman to think of God as an almighty Monarch, ruling the world as from without. We are aware that this, the child's conception of Him, does violence both to His spirituality and infinitude. If He is without the world, He is bounded by the world, and is limited by space; if, again, He is so limited, He is not a spirit, for a spirit transcends the limitation of space. God is the boundless Here, as He is also the everlasting Now. And again, God's omnipresence may give us the key to that puzzle concerning His relation to the so-called laws of Nature, which has sorely exercised many simple but truly pious minds. Science tells us that these laws are changeless and inflexible: the rain and the drought of to-day depend upon the drought or rain of a million yesterdays, and both condition the physical character of to-morrow. But a simple trust in God's omnipotence as constantly rebels against these assertions: religion and science seem opposed. Now, if we would but more habitually remember that the laws of nature, whether of the rain or wind or human health and disease, are God's laws; that they are in no profane or unreal sense part of Himself, the expression of His will and of His being, we should at once see that they are obviously changeless and eternal even as He. To ask God to change them means to ask God to change Himself, to make the rational irrational, the immutable reality a varying and deceptive chimera.

The doctrine of God's omnipresence looked at in this way seems to reconcile us to the at first somewhat hard and terrible conception of universal and changeless law. God is in the world we must believe, and however difficult it may be for us to realise this, we can yet soon begin to understand that the relation of God to the external world is not only made more intelligible upon this hypothesis, but that nature herself, so regarded, assumes an aspect more beautiful and more divine. This is what Goethe felt in the oft-quoted lines :—

> Were *He* a God, who working from without,
> His hand extended, turns the world about?

> No! from within must He that world control,
> Nature in Him, Himself all nature's soul,
> So that what in Him moves and breathes and lives,
> May never lack the power His spirit gives.

And it is the conception of God's immanence, of His Spirit as operative in nature as well as in man, which has constituted the meaning and worth of nature, as the living raiment of Deity, to many a philosopher and poet. It is this conception which, for example, underlies that famous passage in Wordsworth, where he says :—

> I have felt
> A presence that disturbs me with the joy
> Of elevated thoughts: a sense sublime
> Of something far more deeply interfused,
> Whose dwelling is the light of setting suns,
> And the round ocean and the living air,
> And the blue sky, and in the mind of man :
> A motion and a spirit, that impels
> All thinking things, all objects of all thoughts,
> And rolls through all things.

A further useful reflection upon this aspect of our doctrine is that every advance of science is an advance in the knowledge of God, and of His manifestations of Himself in all the universe of things. Yet this reflection, I admit, is double-edged, for God, as we affirm, is reason, and God is love; and this Divine reason and Divine love are fused into a perfect unity. We only distinguish them in our thought as two aspects of an indivisible whole. But whereas, under the discoveries of science, nature may more and more appear as the manifestation of reason, it is very difficult to see that it is also the manifestation of love. Man, indeed, even without science, has

> trusted God was love indeed
> And love creation's final law—
> Though nature, red in tooth and claw
> With ravine, shrieked against his creed.

And if God is everywhere, He is present amid all the horrors and cruelties of nature, as well as in her beneficence and beauty; present in the earthquake and the raging volcano, as well as in the sunshine and the glory of stars; present in the wastes of the wilderness, as well as in the fertility of forests and fields. Is not, then, all nature a mere evolution of chance, unrelated and indifferent to all moral distinctions, rational perhaps, but with a reason that has no resemblance or relation to love? So we come back and come down to our sorest doubt, and the doctrine which was to reconcile us with science and bring us nearer to God has seemingly opened the door to atheism and denial. But to reach the fuller faith we must pass through the gulfs of doubt. We refuse to believe that only in man is reason allied with goodness, and thought associated with love; we refuse to believe that the infinite reason, without which our's would not be, is devoid of those very qualities which are the highest manifestations of our own. If human reason is God's, human love is God's also, nor do we divest God of His responsibility for nature by regarding Him as without nature. God is everywhere and God is one; these two fundamental dogmas of our faith combine and coalesce. And one as He is in His reason and His love, so must all things visible and invisible find through Him and in Him their ultimate explanation as rational and as good.

But now, coming down from these heights

of philosophy, let us think how the doctrine of God's omnipresence may help us in our religious life of every day. The religious aspiration of man seems to express itself in the desire to draw, as we say, nearer to God. Or, again, it is expressed by the desire to become, as we say, like God. What is the link of connection between man and God? How does man draw near to Him? If God were far off locally, if He ruled the world from without, it would indeed seem as if there could be no bridge built between the creature and his God. But when God is conceived as omnipresent and immaterial Spirit, the infinite and yet self-conscious Spirit of Reason and Love, there seems to be at once a possible connection between Him and any other self-conscious nature which is, in however feeble a degree, both rational and good. The more wisdom and goodness you have, the more you know of God, whether you profess belief in Him or not. And, above all, Love is known of love, and the secret of God, so far as man may learn it, is with those who love Him.

But then if God is everywhere, is He equally near to all? If, in the physical world, we were bound to admit that God was in the raging storm as well as in the fertilizing sunshine, must we, in the moral world, say that he is equally near to the sinner and to the saint? We may observe, however, that in the moral world, far less than in the physical world, do conceptions of space and time apply to God. He whose life exhibits less goodness has less of God than he whose life exhibits more. But nevertheless we do assert that the presence of reason is never, and can never be, wholly divorced from the presence of goodness, and that, therefore, in every rational being there is, just because God is omnipresent, the potentiality of a higher life. And so, too, we see from the twin doctrines of God's unity and omnipresence that modern Judaism does well to reject the conception of a devil, that is of reason without goodness, or of a hell, that is of a place or of a state where God is not, though reason is. Just because reason and goodness are inseparably united in God's perfect yet infinite unity, so do we refuse to believe that any soul can ever be lost finally to Him, or that any finite reproduction or incarnation of the infinite self-consciousness will not ultimately be both rational and good.

Once more. God is everywhere: there is no violent separation to be made between the natural and the spiritual. It is *in* the so-called natural that the spiritual must be revealed. So it is not only one day in seven which should or need be dedicated to God, but all days, not one place only, which may be sanctified by His presence, but every place. Not merely in the synagogue, or the church, but in the home, and the school, and the Parliament, yes, and in the workshop, the manufactory, and the mart, is that abiding presence, which can be realised by that which is akin to it, realised by reason, and realised by goodness, but only realised because it is *there*. For if God were not with us everywhere, we could neither be rational nor good. He is the spiritual atmosphere which conditions our spiritual life. And where God is, nothing is wholly trivial or vain. Everywhere, and in all circumstances, we can seek to find out and to follow after His nature and His will, for under all seasons and conditions, God's law, which is the revelation of Himself, the law of reason and the law of love, remain immutably the same. God is the basis and God is the goal.

But yet though we conceive that in one sense God is near to us in our frailty and sin, because love is compassionate and wise, and desires the salvation of all, and because, too, we have the power through God's Holy Spirit to repent and to return, nevertheless we are aware that the wilful obscuration of reason, which is sin, makes us far from God, though He (strange antinomy!) be not far from us. As the most essential attribute of God is goodness, so is moral evil that which prevents us from realising the Omnipresent God. Hence this doctrine of omnipresence serves to magnify and accentuate the unnaturalness and horror of sin. To him who could fully realise the fact that he was living in God's presence, it would be almost impossible to do anything which would sully the clearness of that perception, or would loosen the bond which consciously unites him to God. "Make us realise Thy presence" is therefore the most fundamental of human prayers; and though the Divine omnipresence remains in one sense a constant factor, we shall never cease to echo the aspiring cry of the Psalmist: "Cast me not away from Thy presence, take not Thy Holy Spirit from me."

Once more, the doctrine and conviction of God's omnipresence seem to give a better meaning to suffering and sorrow and pain. If, in the words of our text, we cannot escape from God's Spirit, it is also true that we cannot escape from His love. The one is as universal as the other, because the second is the manifestation of the first. Believing in God, we are led on to trust in His goodness, though appearances may belie it. Suffering and sorrow are means to an end (though the end will never be understood, for only God can know the fulness of His own will), nay more, they are *His* means, and through that one word their horror is lessened, and their poignancy assuaged.

The doctrine of the omnipresence serves, moreover, another purpose still. The God of childhood, the external God who has His dwelling in heaven, is bound to rule the world upon the lines of a benevolent Monarch, that is externally. He distributes reward and punishment, and these allotments of praise and blame are external to, and separate from, the actions or dispositions which were their cause. But the Omnipresent God cannot be conceived as rewarding or punishing externally. His rewards and punishments are internal, that is, they are the necessary concomitants and issues of the action and the character of man. If to draw near to God is man's true happiness, and to be withdrawn from Him is man's true misery, then we have here an ultimate or supreme standard by which to measure the true worth and glory of our lives. It would be mere verbiage and cant to maintain that so lofty a doctrine will satisfy us at all times of trouble, or explain for us all the varied phenomena of human misery, but, nevertheless, the mere acknowledgement of its ultimate truth will constantly help us to "endure and to renounce"—the epitome of man's duty according to Epictetus—constantly help us to overcome that exaggerated importance of individual happiness which, natural and necessary though it be, tends to make us regard the problem of life's destiny as more insoluble, and the love of God as more inscrutable than either of them in reality need be. Of all the proverbs in our language, the one that "Virtue is its own reward" is perhaps the truest and most divine.

Thus God's omnipresence makes us believe not so much that the problem of sin and evil *will* be solved in futurity *to us*, because in no future state of being is it rational to suppose that a finite consciousness will fully understand the infinite purposes of God, but that in the timeless consciousness of Deity the problem is *solved now*, that the everlasting arms are adequate to support their burden.

Suffering is educational rather than punitive, and even in the midst of it we are not deserted of God. "If I make Hades my bed, Thou art there"; there is no darkness so thick which the Spirit of God cannot penetrate, no misery which cannot be borne if it lead us nearer to Him. And is it not a matter of experience that the greatness of man has been proved and evoked by suffering and trial? Is it not a mere fact that for many ages there have lived and died men and women who, by the purity of their lives and souls, have been able to see in suffering not the vindictiveness but the goodness of God—men and women who would freely and soberly confess that it was the very sharpness of their trouble which had brought them closer and closer to God. When sorrow, as we say, does not soften, when it does not reveal God but obscures Him, or when suffering means degradation and sin and ignorance and undeserved defilement, then, indeed, we are tempted to murmur; then, indeed, we need all the faith which we can muster; all our certainty of human love to make us cling yet closer to its Divine original; but while the ordinary human suffering, through which we *can* become better if we do but choose, while only this suffering befalls us, it were unworthy of the best traditions of our humanity if we quailed before the blow. "If Hades be my bed, yet Thou art there."

And thus our doctrine of God's omnipresence, which at first seemed somewhat abstract and barren, may yet have a very real relation to our lives, and may help us to lead them worthily. It gives to life a wondrous dignity; it gives to virtue a peculiar glory; to sin a tenfold horror. It sustains us in trouble; it comforts us in suffering; it imparts to us hope and strength when we have erred and gone astray. "It is never too late to mend," says the hackneyed adage; "It is never possible to lose God," says its religious equivalent. And if this dogma of God's omnipresence may enable us to live more worthily, calling out our full capacities, meagre though they be, of hope, of faith, and of love, will it not also enable us, when the need has come, to die worthily, too? For death itself cannot separate either ourselves or those we love from God: He has given, He has taken, blessed be the name of the Lord! For, though flesh waste away, God is still our portion and their portion; and if His love and His wisdom are manifested in life, they must also be manifested, whatever and however may be the outcome, in that passage and change which we speak of as death. Those we have honoured and loved must die, perchance in the spring-time of their youth, perchance in the fulness of their age; an instant more, an instant less, in God's sight it makes no difference. They pass, but they are with Him, even as we: nay, perhaps, we may say more truly, both of them and of ourselves: They are with God, where we, too, soon shall be.

HOLINESS.

" Ye shall be holy, for I the Lord your God am holy." [1]

I AM not going to consider what the conception of holiness may have been which was in the mind of the writer when he composed this famous injunction. There are few words the changing character of whose history it would be more fascinating to trace than that of holiness. Many interesting articles and monographs have been written on the Hebrew word Kadosh, and perhaps a still more interesting treatise could be compiled which would discuss the comparative history of the idea of holiness and of the

---

[1] Leviticus xix. 2.

words which describe it in several languages and religions. Both the Hebrew word "Kadosh" and the English word "holy" belong to that happier class of words the meaning of which has gradually improved, passing from the material to the spiritual, from the outward to the inward. In Hebrew, Kadosh had a strictly ceremonial and ritual origin; that object was "holy" which had any connection with the service of God, and that man was in a condition of holiness who was ritually entitled to draw near, physically near, to the awful presence of Deity. Thus, in the codes of the Pentateuch we often find the attribute of holiness connected with the avoidance of certain prohibited foods, so that it there becomes a purely outward and material quality. In the celebrated passage from Leviticus, which I quoted as my text, it is probable that an ethical as well as a physical connotation was implied; but, however this may be, the word holy, at the present time and for ourselves, has entirely passed away from the outward and material sphere, and is centred in morality and spiritual religion.

But when we have said this, we have really said very little.

The word "holy" is among the vaguest terms in our vocabulary. If we were asked, not even to give a definition of holiness—for a definition is always a terrible affair—but just to describe the kind of person whom we should consider holy, or to enumerate the qualities which make up the idea, we should probably not only give halting, but very divergent replies. Some of us would be almost inclined to banish the word from modern usage. That would be a great pity, I venture to think, for if you banish the word, you will neglect the thing. Or ask yourselves this question: Do you know any holy men or women among your own friends or acquaintances, and what are their common characteristics? Even so, several people, I fear, will be likely to doubt whether holiness is not a quality which has passed away from our nineteenth century society. For the honour of our generation, let us pause before we accept so mournful a conclusion. Perhaps our hesitation may be rather due to an imperfect realisation of what holiness is, to certain vague and mediæval associations which still hover around this strange and perplexing word.

Let me now proceed to give you the description of holiness which I have so far been able to puzzle out for myself, warning you before I begin that I have no guarantee for its accuracy, and above all that my conception of holiness is probably in many respects very unlike the conception of it framed by the author of the 19th chapter of Leviticus. Nevertheless, there is, I think, a certain amount of meaning still to be given to the term, and the command, "Be ye holy," may still fitly represent an ideal of religious aspiration.

"Of religious aspiration," be it noted. For this will probably be granted by all, that the quality of holiness is intimately associated with religion. Needless to say, I use religion here in no restricted sense. But not only in its past history, but as a matter of present usage, religion may justifiably claim holiness as its own. Now there is no such thing as a religious man who is not good: it is a mere perversion of the word religious, a degradation of it, to conceive the possibility of such a contrast; but you may, and sometimes do, have a good man who is not religious. Religiousness implies goodness, but goodness does not imply religiousness. I now go a step further, and say, though I shall have no time to prove it, a man cannot be holy and not religious, but he may be religious and not holy. You will perceive by this that, as regards the human character, I take holiness to be the crown or efflorescence of religion; or, in the words I used before, for the character of the individual, holiness is the ideal of religious aspiration.

If this be so, no more suitable command in the forefront of religious law than "Ye shall be holy." But once more we are confronted with the old difficulty. Holiness may be the essence of religiousness, but we are still a long way from knowing what it is. How are we to become holy? If we are bidden to be generous or to be kind, we know pretty accurately what the command intends us to be and to do. We know that there are many opportunities open to us all in which to practise generosity and kindness. If we desire to become generous and kind, we are perfectly aware that it is within our power to set about the task to-morrow, or even to-day, and if we fail, it will be through want of will, and certainly not from lack of knowledge. But this airy quality of holiness seems to elude our grasp. Does it resemble those motives into which, as Mr. Casaubon said, we must not inquire too curiously? Will it become feeble in the utterance?

So much is, I think, plain, that if holiness be the flower of religion, and religion itself be based upon morality, the component elements which go to make up the quality of holiness will be partly ethical and partly religious. And all that I here propose to do is to make a little catalogue of these elements, by the help of which we may, perhaps, be enabled to bring the command of Leviticus within the reach and compass of our own ordinary and every-day lives.

It may seem a small matter to begin upon, but to my thinking the first and indispensable preparation for holiness is modesty. The conceited man will never become holy, for self-satisfaction does not consort with the recognition of an ethical and religious standard of which the individual falls hopelessly short. The conceited man thinks that he is perpetually hitting the nail upon the head; the holy man is not, as a rule, thinking about himself at all, but when he does, his thought is instinct with humility. And as a man cannot be religious who is not moral, so, in any proper sense of the word, a man cannot be religiously humble who is intellectually and ethically vain. The holy man puts a real meaning into the familiar prayer, "What are we, what our piety, what our wisdom, what our might?"—whereas the conceited man, on the contrary, is inclined to consider his might, his wisdom, or his piety as a very real quantity indeed. Now if this be so, if conceit is an effectual bar to holiness, holiness becomes, in its very first requirement, a perfectly practical virtue. For this, at all events, we ought each of us to be able to achieve, to crush out and exterminate this vile and foolish quality of conceit.

Perhaps, moreover, there is no time when it is more important and more easy to set about doing this than during our four years at the University.[1] The man who leaves the University conceited may very likely carry his conceit with him to his grave; the man who leaves it modest will in all probability remain modest throughout his earthly career. My own experience was that, at the University, conceit was a stumbling-block to all improvement, so that the young man who came up with, let us say, the purely social or conventional defect of bad manners, lost them rapidly if he was modest, while if he was conceited they stuck to him through thick and thin. The vain young cad remains a cad all the days of his life. But if we have our eyes fairly open, it should be easy to acquire humility at College. Most of us soon find our level there, and most of us must get to know a number of people, both among our contemporaries and among our seniors, so markedly

---

[1] This sermon was preached in the Cambridge Synagogue.

superior to ourselves in all sorts of ways, and yet themselves very often distinguished by simplicity of manners and modesty of thought, that the nonsense, as the saying goes, should effectually be stamped out of us. Believe me, no spiritual progress, no unaffected love of God—in fine, no holiness is possible for us, so long as conceit, which is only a phase of selfishness, stands in the way. And even if there be among you a man of exceptional power, he also can be as humble as the rest. The other day a lady told me she had been talking to Mr. Burne Jones, and she said, "When you see that wonderful collection of your own pictures in Regent Street, Mr. Burne Jones, do you not leave the building with a feeling of proud and delighted satisfaction?" He looked at her, she told me, and said quite simply, "I assure you, most emphatically, that I have no such feeling at all. I only feel how I always, more or less, fail to express the ideal which is within me." When we know that such men as Burne Jones, Darwin, Gordon, each in their several spheres of excellence, can attain humility, it should surely not seem difficult for any one to annihilate conceit, and thus to make the soil of his soul prepared for the growth of goodly seed. Till the rank weed of conceit is eradicated, the flower of sanctity can never blossom and bloom.

I said just now that conceit is only a phase of selfishness, and it would seem as if unselfishness were also one of the necessary qualities which holiness may be considered to imply. So that here again we get a definite virtue to aim at, a definite vice against which to watch and fight. Of course, it may also be said that unselfishness is merely another word for goodness, seeing that the love of self is the root of all evil, so that we have only exchanged one vagueness for another. But this is exaggerated. And in addition to the ordinary ethical unselfishness—about which I need not say another word, for we all know where the shoe pinches on that score—there is what I call a sort of religious unselfishness to which ethical unselfishness may lead the way.

This kind of unselfishness is undoubtedly a

very difficult thing to acquire, indeed, to many of us, perhaps to most, it has little significance. And they to whom it has a full meaning already, to some extent, possess it. Its beginning is trustful resignation to the will of God, and a ready acceptance of sorrow and disappointment, suffering and failure, not merely as the inevitable incidents of humanity, but as transfigured and partially explained in the light of God's purpose and providence. If a man can come to feel that the only true satisfaction possible to him is the consciousness of having, as he believes, not thwarted, but furthered the will of God, of having, as we may say, put himself, so far as his infinitesimal powers will allow, in line with the Divine activities of goodness, beauty and truth, he must, I should imagine, also gradually learn to perceive with growing distinctness that his own mere earthly self is of no importance or account whatever, but that if he represent the smallest speck of grease which enables the coach of human society to run more smoothly, he has received more than his due, and that what *is* valuable in him is the element which unites him to God and lifts him above every thought of personal ambition and every phase of individual desire.

It has been beautifully said by a great teacher, that we may think of any useful work upon which we are engaged, as the work of God upon earth, which is carried on independently of us, but in which we are allowed to bear a part.

And he goes on to say, "It wonderfully clears a man's head and simplifies his life when he has learnt to rest not on himself, but in God, when he sees his daily life with a kind of intensity in the light of God's presence. Such a man has one single question which he puts to himself, one aim which he is seeking to fulfil, the will of God. He wants to know what is true, or right or good in the sight of God. He does not care about the compliments of friends or the applause of the world, the breath of popular air or favour. He desires to work, not for the sake of any of these things, but for the sake of the work only. He wants to be rid of self in all its many deceitful, ever-recurring forms, that he may be united to God and the truth."[1] And if these words, simple though they be, are too much for us, let us translate them into terms of morality, and attempt from that basis to reach the level of religion. And thus we may say: Holiness cannot become the attribute of that man who cares greatly for the world. He must not only set a low value upon mere material things, except as instruments and levers, but he must also be indifferent to renown and applause. He must school himself to that indifference, and yet find in spite of it a motive, equally efficacious and far more educational, to enable him to do his very best, to "succeed" even, if you like to put it so, in that work which his circumstances or his choice have set before him to accomplish. The true servant of God must divest himself of the last infirmity, he must fling ambition away, and accept instead of it the free bondage of duty and the will of God.

---

[1] From a Sermon by the late Prof. Jowett.

Thus the conditions of holiness have taken us over a wide range, yet before bringing them to a close there are two others I would fain mention, the one a definite and clear cut requirement within the reach of all, the other not less real for a few, but rather an aspiration than a command.

Among the words which have become ennobled by time, there is one, lying on the very borderland which separates morality from religion, which seems to possess a mysterious kinship with both. That word is purity. When the Psalmist prays for a pure heart, and declares that he whose heart is pure may stand in God's holy place; or when it is said in the Sermon on the Mount that the pure in heart shall see God, it would in all cases be difficult to say whether a purely moral or also a religious quality is intended. And there is one especial department of human life wherein the virtue of purity reigns supreme, which in all ages both religion and morality have claimed as their own. Even the peculiar superstitions which surrounded it in ancient times, superstitions which were the primary cause of its association or connection with religion, even these, perhaps, partly rest upon some unconscious instinct of the awakening mind that man was in the presence of a mystery deeper than his powers could fathom.

And we have in it a perfectly definite demand, worthy of our greatest efforts, if effort is needed, and an absolute condition of holiness. It is a duty which is incumbent upon us all, rich and poor, wise and foolish, small and great; and to make that universality of obligation fair, it is a duty which, some in one way, and some in another, some with the help of prayer, and some by the inner law of beauty and self-restraint, some with ease and some with difficulty, may bow to and fulfil. This particular temptation we may all vanquish: this particular hindrance to holiness we may all of us overcome. To be a man, says Dr. Fairbairn in a great sermon on watchfulness, which would do everybody good to read, is to bear God's image, and to be like the image we bear. "To be a man is to be chivalrous in thought, pure in feeling, honourable in conduct, true in speech. A man is marked by certain great ignorances; he can dare to be ignorant of the meaner, the more prurient and vicious things of life. In his presence the unclean tale will die on the unchaste tongue, round him will be an atmosphere through which the unclean jest will refuse to travel; he will shut up the unclean book; he will courageously be ignorant, that he may be innocent, of vice. There is a cant of religion, but there is a commoner and meaner cant of irreligion and impurity. He who is a man thinks of every woman through his mother or through his sister, and holds the thought that would tarnish any an insult to those he most reveres and loves." Let this, then, be our ideal:

> "White and clean,
> Outside as inside, soul and soul's demesne."

And now we come to the last of the qualities which make up holiness according to my conception of it—a conception which may indeed be logically faulty and numerically insufficient.

But before I speak of it, let me sum up to you the conditions which have gone before. We saw, then, that the bitterest enemy of holiness is the worship of self, whether in the form of intellectual conceit or moral satisfaction. Selfishness, both ethical and religious, must be rooted out to make room for true humility, and even ambition must yield to unconditional acquiescence in God's will on the one side, and an eager zeal to fulfil it, so far as man can recognise its bidding, upon the other. Holiness needs, moreover, a certain aloofness or detachment from the world, in that sense in which it has been said that it is better to live above the world than to live in the world, a sense which, needless to say, involves no assumption of superiority or of melancholy, and no neglect of every day duties or of social and business obligations. Then, too, holiness implies purity, in body and soul alike, that perfect sanity which in one aspect may be regarded as the exhibition of man's true nature, in another as the triumph of reason, and in a third as the manifestation of God. With the help of these virtues, experience and history have found it to be possible for man to advance to the knowledge and the fruition of spiritual realities. And it is the knowledge and fruition of these realities, in other words, the communion with God, which is the highest and fullest expression of holiness. There are people to whom the spiritual world is more real than the visible world of sense, and who live habitually, if I may say so, in the presence of God. We can scarcely hope to reach their level, and yet *their* achievement may be the goal towards which we strive. If we could find out how it is that God is more real for them than He is for us, or that the secret of God's communion has been revealed to them, we should find, I think, not necessarily that they are more believing than we are, but, quite simply, that they are better than we are, more unselfish, more humble, more pure. They are less tainted of the world, less ambitious, more surrendered to duty and to God. Perhaps, too, they have sought more carefully by the help of prayer to maintain the continuity of spiritual life even through dark days of difficulty and of doubt. Let us then in all these ways and by all these methods attempt to imitate them, and if we are earnest in that attempt, it may be that we, too, in spite of lapse and of sin, may yet find the peace of holiness before we die. For if on the one hand man has recognised in the command "Thou shalt be holy" the bidding of God, he has also perceived that a greater power than his own will sustain him in the struggle for its fulfilment. And therefore, together with the stern injunction, "Thou shalt be holy," which man addressed to his own conscience in the name of God, he has also uttered the prayer of faith, "Create in me a pure heart, O God: and renew a steadfast spirit within me. Cast me not away from Thy presence, and take not Thy holy spirit from me." For the holy spirit of God is the origin, the cause, and the condition of the holiness of man.

RELIGIOUS LIBERTY.

I TAKE for the text of this sermon the seventh verse of the forty-second chapter of the Prophet Isaiah, but as that verse is closely connected with the six verses that precede it, I will read out to you the whole seven verses in their order :—

"Behold ! my servant, whom I uphold, mine elect, in whom my soul is well pleased ; I have put my spirit upon him, he shall cause the law to go forth to the nations. He shall not cry nor clamour, nor cause his voice to be heard in the street; a crushed reed he shall not break, and a dimly burning wick he shall not quench ; truthfully shall he cause the law to go forth. He shall not burn dimly, neither shall his spirit be crushed, till he have set the law in the earth, and for his teaching the countries wait. Thus said the God, even the Lord, He that created the heavens and stretched them forth, that spread forth the earth with the things that spring out of it, that giveth breath unto the people upon it, and spirit to them that walk through it; I, the Lord, have called thee in righteousness, and taken hold of thy hand, and will keep thee, and will appoint thee for a covenant of the people, for a light of the nations; to open blind eyes, *to bring out captives from the prison, and those who sit in darkness from the house of restraint.*"[1]

Now, notice to whom the text words were addressed. They were spoken to men in banishment, to unhappy exiles from their native land, from whom the great possession of liberty had been torn forcibly away. The auditors were therefore materially and politically unfree. But that is not all. The Prophet, as is usual with him in moments of loftiest inspiration, uses words which have a true literal meaning as applied to the facts of the time in a metaphorical manner for spiritual ends. He means that the bulk of the Jews in Babylon were not only languishing in political slavery, but were also suffering from a spiritual bondage of far deeper and graver significance.

The object of this sermon is to ask what profitable and true meaning may now be given

---

[1] Prof. Cheyne's translation.

by us to the words bondage and liberty as applied to religion. In the text passage we have the earliest use of this application. It is deeply interesting to trace the origin of a great thought, and one listens to its earliest and as yet inadequate expression with feelings of reverence not unmixed with awe. In an historical lecture, the business of the lecturer is to explain, as far as he can, what the nascent idea precisely implied to the mind of him who first gave birth to it. But as our business here is not historical, I shall not ask what did our prophet mean by the words " house of restraint " and " the prison," but what meaning may *we* give to the idea of religious freedom after that idea has had more than two thousand years in which to become definite on the one side and to expand upon the other. If we can attach any meaning to it, of a kind not wholly vague and irrelevant to the life of every day, we may also discover whether among ourselves there are any worthy to receive that high title of Servant, or living that life of free bondage unto God whereon the spiritual progress of the world depends.

What then is religious freedom? What is the meaning of liberty?

There are words in the dictionary, which, though they do not fall within the category labelled sacred, have yet the stamp and savour of holiness. Among these words Liberty is assuredly one. Before the word of Liberty it is right to bow our heads in reverence. Nor need the fact that much nauseous nonsense has been written, and many foolish, cruel and wicked deeds have been wrought in the name of Liberty, preclude us from regarding it as one of the noblest words in our vocabulary. Where is Liberty not desirable and desired? In political life, in commerce, in society, in religion, we welcome its advent. A free Parliament, a free press, free trade, free combination of labour, free opinion and religious freedom—all these are good things which we enjoy in the free country of England. But nevertheless the very glory of liberty has cast a sort of halo about it which has often prevented men from knowing it for what it is. Liberty has been regarded as an end, whereas in reality Liberty is but a means. Liberty is a means to a noble life; it is not that noble life itself. But it is the life which is the end, and not the instrument to its attainment. Consistently with this mistake, and from other causes, many men have been content to define Liberty negatively, rather telling us what it is not than what it is. Some will tell us that Liberty is the absence of restraint; others that Liberty is doing as you like, the execution of your own will. But that is merely negative liberty. The free responsible life cannot be realised without this negative absence from restraint, and every social as well as every individual activity demands a free sphere for its development. But the end is not that all men should do as they like, but that all men should like that which it is best for themselves and for others that they should do; and therefore even as regards the action of the State (which is limited in positive directions by various considerations, upon which we cannot enter here), men are beginning to realise that true liberty is not merely negative, or confined to the abolition of restraint; and that it is incumbent upon the

State to make some provision for the attainment of that higher and more positive liberty, where each man shall be free by outward circumstance and inward impulse to live that life which is the fullest expression of his common human nature and his particular individual endowment.

Passing now to our more immediate subject, Liberty in Religion, we shall find that here, too, there is a negative as well as a positive side to the conception. The negative aspect need not detain us long. Religious liberty in the negative sense is assured us by the State, and in England we are so used to its operation, that we regard it as a matter of course. It is history which teaches us what struggles went to its achievement. That belief is free, that men may worship in the manner which suits them best, that religious opinions carry with them no civic disqualifications, these are the familiar elements of negative religious liberty. It is so easy to be satisfied with negations, and those ideas are so much the pleasantest of which we can recognise their excellence as from without, and which make no demand upon our individual effort, that it is not surprising that to most of us the conception of religious freedom does not rise beyond this comfortable negative level. Nevertheless we are only upon the threshold; the hall of liberty is as yet untrodden.

The liberty which stood as an ideal before the mind's eye of the Jewish Prophet in Babylonia was not within the power of the State to grant or to refuse. Positive religious liberty can be given us by no man; it can only be attained by humble effort of mind and will, and through the unceasing agency of Divine love. Tentative and partial must be our definition and account of this high spiritual good, because we are now entering on ideas which, while difficult to feel, are yet more difficult to express. The emotional element in religion can but inadequately be translated into the cold medium of words. Moreover in the conception itself there lies this perplexing feature, that it combines within it a union of opposites. For religious liberty is also bondage, and the bondage from which it sets us free is a spurious liberty. To this seeming contradiction the prophet's words bear witness, for he who leads the prisoners from darkness into light is himself a bondman. A solution of the riddle may be found by saying that liberty in the negative and lower sense means the power to do either this thing or that, one or the other of two opposites. On the other hand, liberty in the higher sense we may take to mean the absolute facility and readiness of doing *only* this, or *only* that. Thus moral liberty in the lower sense means the power we have in any given case of pursuing the right course or the wrong. But if we suppose that the power is equal on either side, it becomes a mere toss up whether we shall do the right *or* the wrong. And of such a character we should rightly deny the attribute of freedom. That man in whom the balance between good and evil is so well maintained is but the toy of chance, the slave of the hour. Apparently most free, he is yet really the victim of the cruellest bondage. It is where the power to do the wrong is weaker than the power to do the right that positive liberty begins. The highest praise we can render to any man is to say of him,

"He could not do wrong if he tried." And if we pass beyond the human sphere, and conceive a being who shall be absolutely free, and yet absolutely bound to goodness, we know that we are reaching forward in our thought to Him whom His earthly children have delighted to call "Our Father who is in Heaven."

Thus the fact emerges that in any system where the good is the assumed end, positive liberty includes within it a distinctly ethical element; it implies the power of doing not anything, but only that which it is right to do. So also in one important sense the freer the agent, the easier it is for him to do good and to be good. But this facility of positive freedom is very different to the shallow ease of the self-complacent formalist and man of custom. The difference is noteworthy. The free man in religion or morality lives the high life, and does his deeds of goodness with ease and ready adaptability; but in his doing there is a fire, an eagerness, and an enthusiasm which stamps the facility of his actions with a peculiar character. Though duty is not resisted, it is greatly felt;

nothing is done from mere routine, nothing from respectable conformity, but all in vivid realisation of the meaning of every act, in abandonment to the inspiration of the moment, and yet in conscious subordination of the particular deed to the general end. Above all, nothing is done from pride or for self-glorification, but everything is begun and concluded as regards the self in humility and as regards humanity in love. These points of difference are of vital importance, and it may also be noted that to the free man, while each good act done satisfies the self, there is yet no self-satisfaction. It is felt that the ideal is far beyond the individual power of achievement.

We saw that, in accordance with the double character of liberty, the free man is also in bondage, while the unfree man enjoys a spurious freedom which he mistakes for reality. Thus we have reached this point: to perceive, first, that there is a kind of bondage which is liberty; and, secondly, that there must be a double-facedness in the word self, which must comprise both a higher and a lower self. Now, three main states are possible: First, the higher self may be consciously used as the slave of the lower self. This state is, however, practically non-existent; it can be elaborated in its most perfect form into a theoretic representation of an imaginary Devil, although the conception of the Devil presents no less difficulties to philosophy than to religion. Secondly, the higher self may be so undeveloped and immature that it can cause no inward conflict; this is the condition of those who, in the eyes of the moralist and the sage, while imagining themselves to be free, are yet in bondage. Between this state and the third there lie a number of degrees sufficient to comprehend the large mass of ordinary struggling humanity. Lastly, there is the condition of those in whom the higher self is always ruling, but as a harmony where no opposition between ruler and ruled is consciously experienced. This is the condition of the heroes and the saints.

Moral Liberty implies the idea of bondage to the moral law; Religious Liberty implies the idea of bondage to God.

But God Himself is the Moral Law, vitalised and made conscious: the Moral Law is the will of His Holiness. Therefore, the liberty of religion includes within it the liberty of morality, and transcends it.

Religion feels that its master and goal is in no wise its own creation, but is endowed with a vitality and consciousness which infinitely exceed the consciousness and vitality of His human servants. Religion feels that its Lord is universal in His operations, and responsive in His love. It feels that in the link of spiritual affinity between master and servant, and in the ever continuous divine call which answers to and corresponds with the human aspiration, the sense of distance and the feeling of bondage are lost in the certainty and rapture of liberty and union.

I have spoken of a false bondage and of a true bondage. The false bondage of the prisoners is a bondage to the lower self and to unrealities or shadows. And here it may be objected that as one man's meat is another man's poison, so may one man's shadow be another's reality. Who is to be the judge? So far as the question of taste goes, there can be no judge. The unreality is certainly a reality to the man who takes it for his end. Nor can there be logical proof in the matter. The appeal is only to the wise and to the good, to the men of illumination and inspiration in all the ages. Their opinion on the matter has been fairly unanimous, and what that opinion is is practically known to all of you.

If the false bondage of the prisoners is a servitude to that which is fleeting, unreal, shadowlike, the true bondage of the servant is a servitude to absolute living reality—the realised ideal of the true self. But the bondage is also freedom, because the whole self is utilised. The mistake of asceticism is to imagine that there must always be an inward war within the soul; whereas liberty is a harmony, wherein no parts of the self are mutilated or quenched, but all find their place and serve their purpose.

Religious freedom brings with it a holy content. But it is interesting to notice that there is a regular scale of spiritual progress, from the low satisfaction of the conventional moralist about whom I have spoken before, through a stage of disquietude and agitation, to the higher satisfaction when "service" and "perfect freedom" are equivalent terms. Some calm and holy souls, unruffled by doubt and passion, serene in their trust and perfect in their devotion, seem, indeed, never to have known that intermediate state of difficulty and contest. Most fair and beautiful they are; and loveliest perhaps among them are those whose knowledge is small, whose religious vocabulary is limited, and whose beliefs are childlike and crude, but whose humility and ardour, whose loyal trust and faithful service stamp them as worthy children of the heavenly Father. And scarcely less to be reverenced than they by us who, let us hope, are struggling to be free—the slaves of shadows cannot discern them, the slaves of custom misunderstand them—are those in whose faces is written the record of the fight from which they have come out victorious. They are wise with the wisdom of experience; they are merciful in judgment, for they too erewhile have been in bondage.

But you will ask, How is religious freedom shown? What does it do? As religion is embodied and expressed in moral action, so is religious freedom shown in morality. The ordinary duties of everyday life, the acquisition of a livelihood, the carrying on of a business or profession, the management of a household—one or more of these must be done in one form or another by all of us. Though even the acts of the freeman are different from those of the respectable slave, more different still is the spirit of his actions, the temper and tone of his life. If any one of you were to leave this building, resolved to live the life of the freeman, your neighbours would perhaps not notice any immediate change in habit or occupation. The same work must be achieved, the same business carried on; there might be—I do not say there *would* be—no outward change observable. And yet the change would be real. As regards work, nothing would be done which is mean, ignoble, or unfair; for labour is a service according to the old motto, and is dedicated to God.

For, let us look finally at the characteristics of the religious freeman, and we shall be able, each one for himself or herself, to see the directions in which our lives would be changed and elevated if these characteristics were ours. First of all, as the mainspring and foundation of the whole character, comes the living conviction of the Divine Reality; the intense eager belief in God as Supreme Righteousness and Supreme Love. Hence arises a keen ardour for morality as the seal and witness to the truth of God. Suffering, sorrow and death are of God's bringing, and He knows their uses and their ends. But the smallest meanness, the pettiest vice, the least deviation from rectitude, the least yielding to temptation, the smallest scamping of work, are a violation of the articles of bondage between man and God. They are regarded as at once a breach of freedom and of service, for they do dishonour to the glory of Him in whose service is perfect freedom. Out of this conviction of the living, responding vitality of the Godhead, there come a happy placidity and cheerfulness, with which those of you who are fortunate enough to know any of the enfranchised class are certainly familiar. This feature rises, when required, to a sublime disregard of pain and loss, of danger, and even death in the service of duty and of God.

Then, thirdly, ardent conviction of fundamental truth is accompanied by personal humility. There is always a savour of slavery about conceit; it implies a lack of discernment between ends and means, between the instrument and the cause. And personal humility is necessary for that love of men, the fellow-servants of the common Master, which is another mark of the religious freeman. No man can care very intensely for others who cares very greatly for himself; and a selfish care for self is a real though not always a known and acknowledged accompaniment of mental or spiritual conceit. The freeman recognises in all men the stamp of their divine origin, and his love of man is not narrowed by the flimsy limits of race and creed. In his love for man there lies the witness of his love for God, which may be regarded as his first and last aspiration, the religious framework of his life's action, its source and consummation, the starting-point and the goal.

Little more than a year ago England could still boast of the possession of a hero, who realised my description of the religious freeman. Since England could not, or would not, save him from an untimely death—and yet can the death of so great a servant be untimely?—let England, at least, keep green his memory. How nobly in him were illustrated, in fresh and living reality, those characteristics which I have feebly and hesitatingly set forth this morning. How ardent and eager was his zeal for the accomplishment of duty; how complete and supreme his disregard and contempt of danger and suffering and death; how true his humility before his Master, his independence before man; how passionate his belief in God and in his own faith; how tender and wise his love for aliens in blood and creed. Surely the name of Charles Gordon will live in history, the great hero-saint of an age in which the fire of faith seems burning dimly. In him at least there was lack of neither light nor heat, and his life was a witness to his faith.

Have we wandered far from our text passage? Our Prophet in Babylon meant, perhaps, something different from to-day's interpretation when he spoke of spiritual bondage and spiritual freedom, and yet he meant something fundamentally the same, for the work of the servant was to consist in the dissemination of the belief in the One True and only God. That knowledge is, as we have seen, the basis of religious freedom. I am not aware that the mission with which those of Israel who had eyes to see and ears to hear were then invested has ever since been countermanded or annulled. Are we worthy to take it up and carry it forward? Not by the accident of birth is the right to service won, but by our own effort and our own labour as the sovereign gift of God. Are we seeking to gain enfranchisement by a divine charter? Are we striving to enter as freemen into the City of God?

"YE ARE MY WITNESSES."

"Ye are my witnesses, saith the Lord, and my servant whom I have chosen." [1]

FEW more trite and familiar words than these in the whole compass of our sacred Scripture. Does something of a shudder or sigh of resignation pass over you as you hear me utter them, remembering how often you have listened to that text being given out from Jewish pulpits? Once more, perchance you think, the old round of complacent eulogy and glorification. Well, let us see if anything can be done, by the simplest and strictest analysis, to instil into these familiar words any tincture of novelty.

---

[1] Isaiah xliii. 10.

We gain no good by self-deception. Indeed, as every one would admit, if we put the thing thus baldly, self-deception is positively harmful. On the platform, or in the Synagogue, we may talk grandly about the immortal mission of Judaism, of the great truths committed to our care and still unknown to those beyond our pale; of the silent but mighty influence exercised by us and our religion upon the outer world; and while we speak and while we listen, the phrases seem to have a valiant ring and a noble, if shadowy, meaning; but, when we pass again to our everyday life, everything is much as before, and if we do not confess that the swelling phrases have little relation, as it seems, to the realities in which we work and live, this is only because we do not care to turn the light of criticism and common-sense upon the beloved and time-honoured creations of religious fancy and convention.

Can we, then, no longer, in any real sense, claim to be the witnesses of God?

To the man who conceived the phrase and wrote it some two thousand four hundred years ago, it was charged with pregnant signification. To him the contrast between the religion of his own small race and the religions of all the rest of the world was wide and vivid. The one was wholly true; the others were wholly false. He was exulting in the full possession of a glorious and novel truth. The doctrine of absolute monotheism owes, so far as we can gather, more to the second Isaiah than to any other Biblical writer. If not the creator of it, he yet stood towards it in the same relation as Darwin stands to the theory of evolution, when compared with those of his predecessors, who had occasional fore-gleams and anticipations of the great discovery. Between this conception of the one and only God, who was still, nevertheless, in a peculiar sense the God of the Jews, and the religions of all other races, as he understood or imagined them, how huge the difference! Moreover, a great spiritual and religious revolution, as the Prophet erroneously believed, was on the very point of effective consummation. The restoration of the Jews to Palestine would, under Jehovah's providence, be the sufficient means for leading all mankind to the knowledge of the worship of Israel's God.

The transition from idolatry to universal monotheism was imminent. No need then to ask if more than rhetoric was implied in those words, which but aptly and succinctly expressed their author's meaning: "Ye are my witnesses, saith Jehovah, and the servant whom I have chosen."

Nearly two thousand four hundred years have passed since those words were written. Are we not, perhaps, asking too much even to suppose that they could possibly have any application for us to-day? Is it reasonable to suppose that a description, valid, let us assume, for a race two thousand years ago, would still be valid for the religious community which represents that race to-day?

When I say "for us" I mean for us English Jews here and now.

To the hapless majority of our brotherhood, crushed in the servitude of persecution in Russia and Roumania, it is easy to see that the words "Ye are my witnesses" are still instinct with solemn and satisfying significance. For what religious kinship can there be between them and their oppressors? What can they think of the Czar's Christianity, but that it is one idolatry the more, an idolatry scarcely less fierce, and even more corrupt and more malignant than the idolatries of Syria or of Rome? To them the God of the Russian taskmaster can have no moral or religious likeness with the God of Israel, with that unique and only God, who for His own inexplicable purposes can still chastise, but will ultimately vindicate and redeem His own. Or, if here and there it should be perceived that the impious persecutors are distorting and reviling the religion of Christ, none the less are the Jews God's witnesses, and no whit they—

> Whose life laughs through and spits at their creed,
> Who maintain thee in word, and defy thee in deed!

But while we do not ignore the bonds of religious brotherhood—some also, with whom I sympathise, if personally I do not share their feelings, would rather say, the bonds of race—

which link us to the Russian and Roumanian Jew, it would be idle to suppress or minimise the immensity of the difference between ourselves and them. It is not merely that they are persecuted, while we are free. The spiritual and intellectual air we breathe is different from theirs. Our environment is largely alien; the culture on which we are fed, the myriad influences which surround and educate us, are alien too; Christian and Hellenic, let us say, but still not specifically Jewish.

Even in ethics and religion, very many of us, directly as well as indirectly, owe much to Gentile literature, Gentile teachers and Gentile friends. The gap which separated the Jew from the outside world is for us bridged over in a hundred different places. Again, we are conscious that the Jews have for a long while not played, and are not now playing, any important part in the religious development of the civilised world. Of what religious influence are the Jews in England? We know that we read and are influenced by the words of great Christian poets and writers, but we are painfully aware that the Christian world is not being influenced by any great writer or poet of ours. We constitute apparently a very small sect, exercising little or no effect upon the great world in which we live. We are moulded and conditioned by it, but it is not conditioned or moulded by us. Nor do we expect or look forward to any sudden upheaval or revolution in the near or distant future which will change our *rôle* from that of apparent supernumerary to that of evident protagonist. Rather do we observe certain seeds of disintegration or decay operating within our own ranks. Such reflections as these are scarcely usual in a sermon preached from the text of " Ye are my witnesses," but I think that unless we take a measure of the difficulties which surround us, we cannot effectually ascertain whether any profitable aspect of truth may still be asserted for us to-day in that famous description of long ago.

Nor are we even yet at the very end of our catalogue. When we are told that we are God's witnesses, and the phrase sticks for a moment or two in our minds, instead of, by mere familiarity, gliding out of them as quickly as water runs off the back of a duck, we are apt to think that if *we* are God's witnesses, and our neighbours are not, we ought not only to believe very differently from them, but to do very differently as well. But here we are confronted with several difficulties. In the first place we are conscious that the old hard and fast labels do not always fit (the continuity of nature comes in, as Mr. Alfred Sidgwick would say), and that the unorthodox Jew, for example, is separated by association and training rather than by conviction and mature belief from his friend the unorthodox Christian. That friend, on the other hand, seems to show no tendency and to feel no desire to change his label, for while his own describes him very imperfectly, he cannot yet see that ours would describe him better. In the second place, our lives are cut according to the same pattern as those of our neighbours, or, if anything, to a somewhat more prevailingly secular type. We do not seem to do, and the large majority of us can never hope to do, anything which would justify the assumption of so magnificent a title as that of witnesses to God. And lastly, we feel that, of all forms of conceit, religious conceit is perhaps the least desirable. For, if not worse, we are scarcely better than our average fellow-citizens, and yet we are inclined to suppose that God's witnesses should be morally and spiritually superior to the world to whom, or before whom, they witness of Him and of His truth.

Here then are our difficulties, our ἀπορίαι. Are they insuperable? Must we in common honesty no longer claim any part or share in the tremendous privilege, "Ye are my witnesses, saith the Lord, and the servant whom I have chosen"?

I do not think we need assess our last two difficulties too highly. It is quite true that the immense majority of us can never be anything but rank and file, but it would be ridiculous to think of an army all generals and colonels. Again, if, for example, England and Italy have certain functions to fulfil in the Divine rule of the world (and believing in God's rule we can hardly deny the assumption), then as Englishmen we may attempt to conceive that function without believing that it is necessarily realised in the individual Englishman, or that the individual Englishman is superior to the individual Italian. But of course the Englishman will be all the more and all the better an Englishman if occasionally, and as opportunity offers, he attempts to express in his own life his conception of what an Englishman should be, to live up to his ideal.

Yet, even in such moments, he will not deny that other nations have their types of excellence, their ideals of national character and function, to which individuals will seek to make their lives conform. And while he will, perhaps, think his own type the best, and certainly be able to distinguish it from those of other nations, he will freely allow that there is a considerable and even growing amount of overlapping in all the higher types with one another. So, too, with religions. If Judaism (I put this forward tentatively, for I am only feeling my way and inquiring with yourselves), still possesses a type of excellence, a specific ideal or function, we need not mind if the contents of that function or ideal partly overlap with those of other religions which are also working for man's welfare and God's truth. For whatever other people may say or do, let us never seek to rival or outbid one arrogance by another; let us hold fast to that dogma which is one of the distinctive glories of modern Judaism: there are many pathways which lead to God.

I may presume, that while none of you would perhaps wholly agree in a detailed analysis of Jewish Theism, you would all agree that this form or phase of Theism, the Jewish religion in other words, is valuable and worth preserving, true, too, within the limits of the human, while capable of adaptation and expansion to the growing needs of the human spirit. You would agree that it is worth preserving, not only as a theoretic doctrine, but also as a practical religion. Now if any of us can honestly say that in spite of lapse and failure and indifference and sin our lives have occasionally, and our characters have partially, been moulded and determined by that Theism, then, I take it, we may without arrogance or hypocrisy assert that we have so far borne evidence to our religion, and in no exclusive, but yet no unreal, sense may claim the title of witnesses unto God. "Ye are my witnesses"; it is quite true that the Prophet did not think there were any other witnesses besides those whom he addressed; we may admit that God has other servants than us, who perchance by His will and in His providence witness to other aspects of His nature and His truth; but because others are, or may be, witnesses in their way, we are none the less witnesses in ours.

It would be idle to maintain that the cause with which Jewish Theism is associated is safely won, that the truths which all of us should agree that it implies are established and secure.

Even if we look at Europe alone we are aware that on the one hand the cause of Jewish Theism is menaced by the foe whom, for our purposes, we may here roughly describe as Agnosticism, and, on the other hand, while not denying the religious truths which Roman Catholicism and orthodox Protestantism and High Church Anglicanism may proclaim, truths some of which may perhaps be insufficiently accentuated and recognised in the Judaism of to-day, it would be false politeness and nerveless tolerance not to remember and to assert that these forms of religion, deviating as they do in some important particulars from the type of Theism which Judaism holds dear and true, are forces subservient in some ways, but yet antagonistic in others, to the propagation and the triumph of our cause.

Still, then, is there need for Jews to hold fast their post and to maintain their charge. The better they can realise it, the more they can live by it, the more truly are they in very sooth enrolled among the servants and the witnesses of God.

Moreover, it becomes us to remember that Jewish Theism is not confined to the somewhat barren and abstract assertion "there is one God." The unity of God has occasionally tended to become a kind of fetish amongst us; it is surely only then a fruitful and helpful doctrine when its implications are adequately explained.

But putting the dogma of the Divine unity to-day on one side, for there is no time to consider it fully, Jewish Theism also includes two other elements or features which are at least as essential to it as the unity of God, even if they partly overlap with the teachings of other Theistic religions. I simply enumerate them here—namely, first, the close relation of religion to morality, in other words, that the pure and good life is the service of God; and, secondly, that one phase of religion is realised in feeling, or, in other words, that the aspiration of the Divine, and the communion with God, are not illusions but realities. These elements of religion are also a portion of that whole to which the life of the Jew may witness.

I have put this part of my case shortly and

baldly before you, and it may seem a tame conclusion at which to have arrived. "What," it may be asked, "is the practical issue? Merely this: 'Be good, be religious;' at the best you give us only an extra sanction for the old, old bidding. And as to the two constituent elements of Judaism, which you have just enumerated, are they not both maintained by Unitarianism and Theism? Are we Jews because we hold them, or because we hold them need we remain Jews?" To which I would reply, that so far as these two elements are held by the Unitarian and the Theist, they are witnesses to God, even as we; but because others hold them as well as ourselves, that is no argument why we should not still claim them as a part of Judaism, or exchange our label for another. They hold them because Jews have taught them, and it is for them to come to us rather than for us to go to them.

To these offshoots of Christianity, which lie nearer to us than to the creed from which they have sprung, we would extend a friendly hand of greeting and recognition

But be sure of this, that the common cause, if common it really be, which we and others have both at heart, will not, as yet at any rate, be benefited by any closer fusion. Even if the difference between a certain section of Jews and the Unitarian or Theist be rather one of name than of substance, still for our part we do well to remember that even a name with a connected history of three thousand years of spiritual development is no meagre power, nor are the millions of living Jews a factor to be despised. I am commonly supposed to be a Reformer, a Radical, and many other disagreeable things, but this I do say advisedly: Beware of losing the support of the past, and of its heritage. If religion and Theism be really dear to you, if you are not inclined to slip away from Judaism, from mere indifference or unbelief, I would urge you to remember that our Theism has been reached amid Christian environment and Christian influences, be it allowed, but on a Jewish foundation, and as a purely Jewish result. Its nourishment, though you may not know it, is largely Jewish too. If you do not cultivate it on its own soil, your Theism may wither, and as a propelling factor in your lives religion itself may even sicken and die. The easy question, "What separates the liberal Jew from the liberal Unitarian or Theist?" may provide a convenient excuse for indifference; it will scarcely of itself lead to spiritual progress, or to a higher and more constant level of personal and individual religion.

It is clear that this sermon, if it appeals or is helpful to any, can only help or appeal to those who have moved away from older conceptions of Judaism under the stress and influence of modern currents of criticism and thought. It is largely upon its power of retaining a religious hold upon such persons that the future of Judaism depends. Let them maintain their Jewish separateness and their Jewish consciousness, and they will be able more and more successfully (for the future is surely theirs) to transform outward Judaism to correspond with their own beliefs. Let them never be tempted by their Christian friends without, or by their orthodox Jewish friends within, to think that they have no right, in a true religious sense, to the name of Jew, no place in the religious brotherhood of Israel. Let them but be patient and brave, and they will gradually (though one generation will not see the issue) stamp their beliefs effectively and effectually upon Judaism as a whole. "Ye are my witnesses," said the Prophet, and with that witnessing he combined a proselytising activity in the highest and best sense of that easily perverted word. And here is a great paradox. It is only they who have had their doubts—but have worked their way through them and beyond them—as to the continued possibility and justification and need of Judaism, who can be, in the Prophet's sense, missionary witnesses to God. It is only they who, as we may believe, will yet make Judaism a light to the Gentiles, that the pure knowledge and worship of God may extend "unto the ends of the earth." It is only they who will, at last, have so fitly furnished forth the sanctuary that they may open the gates, in order that the synagogue of the Jew may be the prayer-house of many nations. It is they who can help most practically to bring to its living realisation the dream of the psalmist seer, so that (not, indeed, of the earthly and material, but) of the spiritual Jerusalem it shall be said, This one and that one was born in her.

We have, then, these facts. The fundamental teachings of Jewish Theism are not yet accepted by the world. To those truths the Jews still bear witness. There is no evidence to show that they would make quicker headway in society if any section of the Jews abandoned their charge and dropped their distinctive being and name. On the contrary, there is reason to believe that their teachings would gain ground if every Jew were keen in faith and active in his adherence to Judaism. Their victory is retarded by Jewish indifference, and more especially by the indifference of those who might otherwise be helping in the great work of transformation and reform. I submit, therefore, in sober seriousness, that to no one more than to the "liberal" Jew do the words of the text, "Ye are my witnesses," fitly and cogently apply. Let it not once more be said of us, as, alas, it was too truly said of the

Israel which returned from Babylon, "Who is blind, but my servant? or deaf, as my messenger that I send?" Let not Israel be compelled to put in a claim to stand for him,

> Che fece per viltate il gran rifiuto.

THE CONTEMPLATION OF DEATH.

"Dust thou art, and unto dust thou shalt return." [1]

MEN of science have much to tell us of nature's regularity. To express the fact that all nature's operations and processes follow and obey with unvarying precision those laws wherein her Creator's will is revealed, they have coined a phrase, the Uniformity of Nature—words of constant recurrence in scientific literature and argument. Not all of you present here to-day may be familiar with the words, but with the fact which the words express, you are so familiar

---

[1] Genesis iii. 19.

that you act upon it at every turn and corner of your lives. You are quite sure that the water in your kettles will boil to-day by the same means that made it boil yesterday; you arrange to take a walk to-morrow morning at ten o'clock, and are perfectly certain that the sun will have already risen to give you light upon the way. It is now June weather and warm, but sometimes you buy your winter frocks and coats in the summer, without the smallest doubt lest the chill and the frost should not recur again. In hundreds of ways, then, we are always acting upon this grand fact or assumption of the Uniformity of Nature.

How far, I want to ask, do we pay heed to it in one instance—as much, without an exception, as the following of winter upon summer, or night upon day—and of the nearest importance and the closest relation to ourselves? How far, I want to ask, ought we to pay heed to it, and shape the action of our lives and mould the disposition of our souls, with more constant and consistent recollection of its inevitable certainty? It is not difficult for you to guess to what instance of the great Law of Uniformity I am referring. You will probably be aware that I am thinking of the end which upon earth awaits us all,—the common end which befalls alike the poor and the rich, the wretched and the happy, the end to labour and enjoyment, to suffering and success, to the good life and the bad,—the end which human imagination has personified so variously, according to its changing mood—now as the pitiless conqueror and now as the gentle deliverer. I am thinking of Death.

Every man and woman assembled here to-day must die. Old and young, the weak and the strong, must be gathered in by that invincible Mower whose scythe never fails to reach his prey. When the hour shall be, whether distant or close at hand the goal, we know not. But try our uttermost we cannot escape. This is a rule unlike the rules of grammar—it has no exception.

When preachers begin to talk of death and the uncertainty of human life, they often fall into exaggerations, and I remember hearing a wise man, whom it is my privilege to call my master, begin a sermon in Westminster Abbey by telling the huge congregation who were intently listening to his words, that he would preach to them that day, not upon the uncertainty, but upon the comparative certainty, of human life, a view, he said, equally true, though less frequently heard from pulpits.

Let us, then, seek to consider, without the exaggeration of rhetoric, what might be the effect of the conviction of death were it more continually before our minds. It will be the prelude to that other inquiry whether we do indeed remember the inevitable fact of death sufficiently, or whether, in other words, the remembrance of death should not have more influence upon our inward and outward lives than to the majority of us we may assume it to possess.

In moments of fresh and vigorous vitality it is not easy to realise death. We can hardly fancy that the time must come, not merely for the old and the weakly, but also for us the young and the healthy, when we too shall have to say to all things upon the earth farewell and good-bye for ever. Good-bye to the sunshine and the flowers, to all the nooks and corners and objects which are familiar to us and endeared —above all, to the people we love. The anguish of this last good-bye—whether in the thought of their death or ours—is mitigated by the belief that somewhere and somewhen and somehow there shall be a meeting for love again. But for all that, though the love may be higher and more wonderful, it will not be the same. We cannot expect to know again the old human weaknesses and oddities, the little peculiarities which gave tone and colour to the beloved personality; we cannot hope to hear again that sweet earthly human laugh, or again to wipe away those tender human tears from the face not fair enough for heaven, and beautiful it may be in our eyes alone.

We believe that behind the veil there may be prepared for us a fuller joy, a grander knowledge, a deeper love; but the very certainty of difference justifies our sadness for the loss of the human felicities that may be lower, but yet are real. Death will take us from the known to the unknown. Of the vision which lies behind it none can learn until for him too has struck the appointed hour.

> Strange, is it not, that of the myriads who
> Before us passed the door of darkness through,
> Not one returns to tell us of the way
> Which to discover we must travel too.

The fact that death may come soon or late, suddenly or after warning, adds to the complexity of the situation, but it also increases largely death's moral significance. I said that death's certainty is sometimes a thought difficult to realise. But it is right to face the facts of life, stern though they be, and now and again to direct our thoughts earnestly towards this great reality may exercise a stimulative and bracing effect upon our moral capacities. But before it can do this, it is not unreasonable or ignoble that the vivid realisation of death should cause a shudder. The mere thought of physical corruption may well make the strongest of us shrink away in horror and awe. You will remember Claudio's words when, for a moment, in the frantic fear of imminent death, he stoops to urge Isabella to save his life by her own shame :

> Ay, but to die, and go we know not where;
> To lie in cold obstruction and to rot;
> This sensible warm motion to become
> A kneaded clod; and the delighted spirit
> To bathe in fiery floods, or to reside
> In thrilling region of thick-ribbed ice;
> To be imprisoned in the viewless winds,
> And blown with restless violence round about
> The pendent world; or to be worse than worst
> Of those that lawless and incertain thought
> Imagine howling :—'tis too horrible!
> The weariest and most loathed worldly life
> That age, ache, penury and imprisonment
> Can lay on nature is a paradise
> To what we fear of death.

How strong the vital instinct is we may sometimes observe in very old people, for whom, as one would imagine, the future had but little to offer and whose chief joy must lie in the memory of past years, apparently still clinging with attachment and even anxiety to life's thin, weak thread. For here again have preachers exaggerated. Life for the majority at any rate is not a mere vale of tears, but includes within it both sorrow and joy, and even the sadness which is past often becomes softened and endeared by the lapse of time.

Nor let us forget or pass over too lightly before we draw the moral, that other aspect of death, no less true and spiritually as valuable. Death the Destroyer is also Death the Deliverer. To all the sorrows and sins, to all the disappointment and failure, to all the suffering and woe of our mortal lot, here is the limit and the end. Looked at in the light of death many of our troubles, just as many of our pleasures, seem paltry and contemptible, while those which are real are more bearable in the thought of their certain transiency. For some whose fortunes upon earth contrast too glaringly with that blessedness of another world in which their faith is very strong and pure, for these sometimes there may seem to lie a deep meaning and propriety in that strange custom of a Thracian tribe which the Greek historian Herodotus has preserved for us. Among the Trausoi, he tells us, when a child is born, the relations sit around it lamenting; they recount the varied ills which flesh is heir to, and the many woes the new-born babe must undergo. But when a man dies, they bury him in festivity and gladness, in that being rid of all human ills he now is happy without alloy.

But if there are some for whom it is a relief to dwell upon the certainty of death's advent, to the majority in every class life is not so sore a struggle that they look forward with longing eyes to the coming of the inevitable end. The very contrary I expect to be nearer the truth. By the majority, by ordinary people like ourselves, living ordinary and humdrum lives — by such as form the overwhelming bulk of those who listen to ordinary sermons like the present—the thought of death, at once the greatest and the most certain fact of existence, is probably too much neglected and put aside. And thus we are once more brought back to our main problem; whether or no a more vivid realisation and a more constant remembrance of death would have any determinable effect upon the tenour of our lives, and whether we ought, by dwelling more frequently and more intently upon this solemn fact, to put it to a better moral purpose before our thoughts upon it are closed by its experience.

Some people might fancy that a more constant recollection of death would be positively harmful. Might it not give rise to the reflection that, since life is short and uncertain, our best plan is to get as much amusement out of existence as we can. The cynical and selfish advice of the sensualist may seem after all the wisest. "Let us crown ourselves with rosebuds before they are withered."

> Ah, make the most of what we yet may spend,
> Before we, too, into the dust descend.

But, as a matter of fact, none but ignoble natures are ever, or have ever been, tempted to put the thought of death to such a use. The nobler souls do, indeed, desire to make the most of what they yet may spend; but, and herein lies the moral lesson of death, they cannot find the satisfaction of achievement in the transient pleasures of sense or in the gratification of purely selfish and individual aims. It is not easy for any of us wholly to crush and stamp out that Divine spark of reason which is alike the cause of all the glory and, by virtue of its environment, of all the sadness that raises mankind above the beast. The very constitution of our being makes it impossible for us to find abiding satisfaction, except in those activities of brain and hand which can hardly be manifested except for social and general ends. And thus the thought of death, in the vast majority of cases, will always tend to diminish, rather than to increase, the selfishness of man.

Again, it might be imagined that the vivid realisation of death's inevitability would tend to exercise a benumbing effect upon human energies; that it would tend to make us live, if not more selfishly, at all events more slackly. Will not the thought of death make sluggards of us, lazy men and lazy women, who will say to themselves, "There is no time in which to work before death overtakes us. How can we arrange our lives according to any rational plan, when at any moment we may be snatched away?

And after all, since each must die, is it worth while to turmoil and to fret; is the game worth the candle? In a hundred years will it not be the same?"

But here, again, such gloomy results of dwelling upon death are contradicted by experience. Compared with the life of the individual, the life of the State, still more that of humanity at large, is of indefinite length, and the wish to contribute to society as much as possible before the summons to depart is heard has probably been a far more potent, as it undoubtedly is a far nobler, motive in the lives of men than the idea that work is useless because every individual is but born to die.

We are thus led to believe that the contemplation of death, apart from theories regarding the life to come in another world, can have, in the large majority of cases, no evil effect upon the moral nature. If, then, its effects are good, what are their characteristics? To know them will also be to know how we may best make use of them in our own lives.

But here a very important difficulty comes in. I am sure that many people who are in the habit of listening to sermons must have often made the following reflection:—"All that you have been saying is very nice and pretty, and even true, but it is unreal and unpractical. You talk as if we were quite free to shape and change our lives as we please. But, as a matter of fact, our lives are to a great extent made for us by circumstances, and we cannot change them even if we would. We work, we eat, we sleep, and we take a little rest, and day after day there is the same routine. We must work to make a living, and we must also eat and sleep in order that we may work, and as for our rest, a walk in the country, a newspaper over a pipe, a game with our children, a chat with a neighbour—that is how we take it. In lives so humdrum and so uniform, is there opportunity for high lessons of morality? The motives which induce us to work are very near and very simple, and the margin of time to be spent as we please, after the claims of work and sleep and appetite have been disposed of, is very narrow. Do not, then, nine-tenths of our lives lie quite outside the range of the preacher's teaching? It may be good, it may be true, but is it practical, is it of value?"

At first sight there seems a very great deal of unanswerable force in these objections. But if we push them to their logical issue, we shall, I think, perceive that there must be a fallacy lurking somewhere in their argument. For do not the objections come to this, that conduct—by which he meant moral conduct—will not take up, as our great poet and critic, Mr. Matthew Arnold, has taught, more than three-fourths, but less than one-tenth of human life? In other and simpler words, Do the objections not imply that the majority of men have scarcely time or opportunity to be either good or bad?

Well, can this be true? Does any man and woman in this building really believe that he or she has it not in his or her power to be either good or bad? Let each one probe his conscience, and reply. We should, I think, all allow that opportunities of different kinds are continually occurring to all of us which we are forced to stamp with a moral character either bad or good. Each one knows best the petty, and yet important, details of his own life, and each one must confess that, even in the most ordinary processes of trade, in the most recurrent operations of the household, there are opportunities for acting well or ill, earnestly or slackly, discharging a duty fully or slurring it over, producing finished work or scamped. And do many days pass, even in the most humdrum and monotonous of lives, in which there is no occasion to swallow a petty insult or forgive a trivial wrong, to make a slender sacrifice, to show some small kindness or render some passing help? No man can live wholly for himself. Each one is brought into constant touch with his fellow-men in a variety of social relations, whether as father or son, as brother or husband, as employer or employed, as producer or consumer. Each one of these relations can be fulfilled well or ill, and each one of them, if we think about it sufficiently, can, and I fancy does, afford not only occasional, but frequent, perhaps daily, opportunities for fulfilling duty or for neglecting it, for being, in other words, either good or bad. Therefore, unless circumstances are very wretched and oppressive—it is the deepest tragedy of human society that for some they are—the man who could honestly say that he has passed a neutral week, a week in which his conduct has never been good or bad—that man is a sinner by virtue of his own confession; he has neglected the great prerogative of humanity, the struggle for goodness, now ending in failure and now in success.

So, if it be true that it is given to all, upon whom the sorrows of life do not press too hardly, to be either good or bad, let us ask, What are the moral uses to which we may turn the contemplation of death?

Preachers have been wont to emphasize the vanity of mortal strivings when looked at from the point of view of death and eternity. "What does a man take with him," said Koheleth, "of all his labour in that last day? Naked as he came, so shall he go, and what shall be his profit for all his toil?" Does there not seem, indeed, a touch of absurdity in our eagerness over this achievement, our vexation at its failure, our pride in its success, when we remember that, in a little while, we must say farewell to all? But the answer rises to the lips: Is death indeed the universal conqueror? Or are there not some things, not made, perchance, of flesh and blood or of aught material, which we believe to be beyond the reach of his control?

There are three qualities of whose eternity we are convinced, because they are summed up, in a single perfect unity, in the very life and nature of God Himself. These three qualities are Beauty, Wisdom, and Goodness; of which Beauty is the least and Goodness the greatest. Now, any life passed in faithful service to these qualities, or to one of them, has, to that extent, broken through the limits of its mortality. And it is precisely in the service of the greatest of these qualities, in the service of goodness, that we all may be enrolled as soldiers. Goodness is immortal in more senses than we can clearly realise, for each additional piece of it, as it were, brings creation nearer to its Lord.

The moral of our tale is this: Live as imperishable a life as you can. Take care that some of it, at all events, eludes the grasp of the Destroyer. Now the service of goodness is shown by the service of our fellow-men, and this service, again, can be expressed in a variety of ways. Humanity, as a whole, is not immortal, any more than the individuals which compose it. The life of Earth, as it had a beginning, so also will it, we may assume, find its close. But that close is so indefinitely distant that, compared with our own lives, the life of human society may be regarded as eternal. In the service of man, we are therefore working for the true and real eternity of goodness and for the comparative eternity of human society. That service is fulfilled, more or less efficiently, in innumerable ways. Not the matter of your work only, but the manner of it decides its imperishable quality. Not only what you do, but how you do it. The tailor who never wittingly sews a loose stitch, the shopkeeper who never wittingly sells short measure or adulterated goods—both these men have added to the store of those eternal and imperishable commodities upon which the true welfare and progress of mankind depend.

But besides seeking to make our very livelihood a true service of man, and a glorifying of God, most of us can find time and opportunity for a still directer service. Society demands that each one of us, so far as he is able, shall do some purely social work, from which he will receive no individual profit. In such work as this lies the escape from death's control. In the service of your town or your community, as well as in the constantly recurring acts of private charity and love, which are the very salt and flavour of all human life, must your repulse of death's assault consist. The tremendous uncertainty of life, nevertheless not great enough to prevent us ordering the plan and disposal of our lives carefully, yet urges us imperatively to lose no time.

A great Roman emperor, perhaps the wisest

and best sovereign who has ever mounted a throne, said, with admirable simplicity, "Do not act as if thou wert going to live ten thousand years. Death hangs over thee. While thou yet livest, while it is yet within thy power, be good."

And now, in conclusion, a few words about the effect of death's contemplation upon the inward life, upon the disposition of our souls. I said before that the ideas of physical corruption and a farewell for ever from earthly things might well cause a shudder of dread and sorrow. But we can pass through this phase of feeling to another and a higher phase beyond it. We have to carry up the idea of death to our idea of God, and then death will lose its terror. Like the Psalmists of old, we must have faith in the absolute goodness of God and in the wisdom of His decrees. Like Epictetus, we must make up our minds to listen happily and contentedly for the summons to depart. If our consciences shall enable us to say in his words, "I have not dishonoured God by my acts," we must be willing to give back the gift of life without a murmur and without fear. Death and life are God's instruments, and for the rest—

> Thou wilt not leave us in the dust,
> Thou madest man, he knows not why,
> He thinks he was not made to die;
> And thou hast made him; thou art just.

But before death comes, its contemplation should plant within the soul elevation and peace. Above all it should make us see things in their true light. For all things which seem foolish in the light of death are really foolish in themselves. To be annoyed because so and so has slighted us, or been somewhat more successful in social distinctions, pulled himself somehow one rung higher up the ladder than ourselves, how ridiculous all this seems when we couple it with the thought of death. To pass each day simply and solely in the eager pursuit of money, or of fame, this also seems like living with shadows when one might take one's part with realities. Surely when death is at hand we should desire to say, " I have contributed my grain to the great store of the eternal. I have borne my part in the struggle for goodness." If the thought of death has helped us so to spend our lives, we may well be thankful. And let no man or woman suppose that the smallest social act of goodness is wasted for society at large. All our help, petty though it be, is needed, and though we know not the manner, the fruit of every faithful service is surely gathered in. Let the true and noble words of a great teacher ring in conclusion upon our ears:—"The growing good of the world is partly dependent on unhistoric acts; and that things are not so ill with you and me as they might have been, is half owing to the number who lived faithfully a hidden life, and rest in unvisited tombs."

THE WAY OF RIGHTEOUSNESS.

"I walk in the way of righteousness, in the midst of the paths of judgment."[1]

You all, I hope, remember the speaker. It is wisdom, wisdom standing "beside the gates, at the entry of the city, and crying aloud unto the sons of men." She bids them listen to her, and she will fill their treasuries, to love her, and they shall inherit substance. And yet that which she gives is better than silver, and her fruitage is nobler than gold. She teaches rulers to reign with equity, and politicians decrees of justice. She is the bond of union between earth and heaven, between man and God. For

---

[1] Proverbs viii. 20.

God possessed her in the beginning; she was the architect through whom the works of creation were fashioned; she rejoiced in the habitable earth, and her delight is in the sons of men.

It is a notable conception, running more or less fully through all the so-called wisdom literature both of the Canon and the Apocrypha. You will observe that wisdom in one of her aspects is identified with prudence—worldly wisdom, as we say in English—but in another aspect she becomes equivalent to goodness, and in a third she is the counterpart of religion. The wise man of Proverbs is not only sensible and prudent, but he is also actively good, and conversely piety implies wisdom.

This close relation between wisdom and goodness can be noticed in many other religions and philosophies. In some of these, it might at first appear as if the sovereign position of morality had been somewhat depressed by being regarded only as the necessary pathway, through which all must go in order to reach the wide field of supremest wisdom that lies beyond.

But, however this may be, the closeness of the union is unmistakeable. The Stoic philosopher, as well as the Buddhist monk, the disciple of Spinoza as well as the follower of Plato, are all good in so far as they are wise, and wise because they are good. And the Rabbinic development of Judaism partially accepted the same teaching. The content of wisdom is, indeed, painfully narrowed and curtailed, but the intellectual element in the conception of ideal goodness was always retained, and the harsh saying of Hillel, "no boor can be pious," seems but the consequence of the theory that wisdom and goodness are inseparable. We know, too, how Plato's master is supposed to have maintained that virtue can be taught, and that having realised the good, it would be impossible to choose the evil.

In all this smoke there must lurk some fire. In other words, there must be a more real relation between virtue and intelligence than we are often willing to concede. For at first sight there seems something positively repellent in allowing even the smallest connection between goodness and wisdom. Nay more, such a connection seems not only repellent but untrue. For cannot the clever man be also a scamp, and, above all, cannot the stupid be also good, and the ignorant pious? To deny this were blasphemy against God himself, who has chosen His witnesses from among the feeble and the foolish and the ignorant, as well as from the learned and the wise. Goodness, we feel, is the privilege of humanity at large, not of a small section of it, and no stories move our admiration and our tears more easily than those which, like Miss Lemon's " Pair of Lovers," tell of boundless love and self-sacrifice among the toiling thousands for whom the page of knowledge has never been unrolled. We humbly thank God, that if, in His inscrutable will, He has thought fit to allow so much crime and ignorance and misery and disease to continue century after century upon the earth, He has also granted to men the capacity to exhibit an exquisite goodness and nobility amid unloveliest surroundings. There is, indeed, a love born of misery and squalor, which is hardly rivalled by the love of comfort and prosperity.

In this sense, then, righteousness is independent of wisdom, and love, both the love of God and the love of man, is supremely disdainful of knowledge. Goodness may go hand in hand with ignorance, and love may be the companion of folly. And goodness and love are greater far than wisdom and knowledge. "If a man would give all the substance of his house for love, he would utterly be contemned."

Is the cause of our text hopeless? Not entirely. Let us see quite simply, how in the first place—it is a very commonplace suggestion but not unprofitable—wisdom can be put to the service of goodness and used as her handmaid.

It is an everyday remark that many a sin, both of omission and of commission, is due to thoughtlessness. It may be the mere forgetfulness of the moment, or it may be a lack of comprehension and intelligence, but in either case how unfortunate, sometimes even how disastrous, is the issue. Who has not felt the sting of sharp remorse, when too late he realises that the right word omitted, or the wrong word said, has caused a needless misconception which rankles, or a needless pain which throbs in the heart of another? Often, too, I am sure, mere obtuseness blinds and deafens us to the wounds we give or to the opportunities for well-doing which we pass by unheeded. I do not mean that we consciously wrap ourselves round in the cloak of indifference—that is another story—but I am talking of our frequent dulness and moral insensibility which it is partly within our power to lessen and drive away. And this leads on to another point closely connected with what has just been said. I am no psychologist, and cannot pretend to determine the intellectual element in imagination, but that there is such an element we shall all allow. And though we are born with different doses of imaginative capacity, still the culture of the imagination, as Mr. Goschen has been again reminding us, is to some extent possible for us all. And who is a more powerful servant of goodness than imagination? It is precisely the lack of it which prevents sympathy and forbearance, or which leads to that mournful and obstinate closing of the eyes to the needs and views of others, when prejudice assumes the aspect of virtue, and narrowness is confused with devotion. A more habitual considerateness, and a more determined exercise and culture of the imagination, would make not only our private, but also our communal life run more smoothly, helping "to turn the heart of the fathers to the children, and the heart of the children to their fathers."

Here we have had two everyday examples how goodness may be enfeebled by lack of intelligence. Taking a wider sweep, we are conscious that if the old saying that man was created in the image of God means anything, it can only mean that there is a kinship, at however great a distance, between the Reason of God and the Reason of man. The divine reason we believe to have two main aspects, an aspect of goodness or love, an aspect of wisdom. But in God these two aspects of reason are only ideally separable: we believe them in Him to have achieved an absolute unity, so that there is no activity of His wisdom which is not also the product of His love. And if in man no such unity as this is conceivable, some relationship must at least be maintained, for reason is an element of goodness, which is not human, if it be not rational.

Looked at from one point of view, goodness seems easy. That is to say, it is not apparently an intellectual obscurity which prevents us from doing right, but rather the obscurity produced by passion and desire. We know the right, and do the wrong. But it is useful sometimes to consider a sense in which goodness is not easy, and to find that it is precisely here where the intellectual and moral elements in our nature must strengthen and develop each other.

From some of the grosser temptations and sins those whom I am addressing to-day are probably able to keep themselves free. We are not likely to murder, steal, swear falsely. But the circumstances of life are far subtler and more complicated than the simple rules of morality laid down, for example, in the various codes of the Pentateuch.

Conflicts of duties arise in which the right path is exceedingly difficult to discern, and though we are often told in churches and synagogues that one can always hear, and always trust the dictates of conscience, we know very well that important decisions have to be taken, or some delicate choice has to be made, in which conscience gives no clear and adequate response, and yet that these are cases which may closely affect the welfare of others, and for this and other reasons, lie well within the province of morality. We are responsible for the *effects* of our actions as well as for their motives, and the excellence of the latter will not compensate for the evil of the former. "I meant well" is the lamest of lame excuses. For example, who would not nowadays acknowledge that almsgiving is only good if done with intelligence, and that the higher charity demands the use of the head as well as the heart? If you give to passing beggars in the street, your motive may be admirable, though it is more probably selfish, but if knowledge and reflection can tell you that you are not lessening the horrible sum of human misery, but increasing it, your admirable motive will go for nothing; your ignorance is culpable. This instance of a union between wisdom and goodness is universally acknowledged; in the future it may be that men will be much more generally condemned than they now are for not weighing the consequences of actions, hitherto, like early and improvident marriages, considered either praiseworthy or at least innocuous.

Again, cases may arise in which the course of action which is undoubtedly the easiest may also seem morally the best, and here it sometimes needs a clear head to disentangle the threads, and to discern whether desire may not be masquerading in the guise of duty. For the misinterpretation of duty has led, and still leads, men and women to the commission of strange errors and pettinesses; and sometimes even personal feelings and private spites have so clouded the mind that actions which have been really dictated by the lowest, have seemed to the doer of them to have been the outcome of the highest and most religious motives which can enter into the human mind. But if such persons had been in the habit of bringing their intelligence to bear upon their conduct, these ethical obscurations might have been avoided. There is no more accomplished juggler than the mind of man. With the most perverse ingenuity it can dress up the worse as the better cause. Therefore the mind must, as it were, defeat its meaner tendencies by its own weapons. As the reason is constantly inclined to enter into the service of our lower desires, and present them in decked-out shapes and elegancies to the moral consciousness for approval and adoption, so must we be ever on our guard to emancipate the reason from this unnatural servitude, and to compel it, if we may so distinguish between our reason and ourselves, to see things and motives as in truth they are, unclouded by passion, by prejudice or by desire.

I have already partly indicated that quick perceptions and intuitions—and these qualities may be cultivated or neglected—certainly do much to make life bearable and increase the store of good. A wise woman once said, "More mischief is wrought by stupidity than by wickedness." At all events, dulness often lets slip many opportunities by which at little cost of time, and very often, one is ashamed to feel, at little cost of trouble, some real, if trifling happiness may be given, some sadness lightened, some misconception cleared away. Have not many of us experienced the thrill of joy that may be felt through a look, a smile, a word, even by a touch of the hand—that touch which may sometimes, as the great George Eliot knew, be the outcome of exquisite instinct and the equal of many speeches? Even in busy lives there are opportunities for kindness and chivalry and love, which those who have eyes to see may perceive and make good use of. Let us be careful that we do not wake up to their existence when the time for them has passed for ever, and when remorse will add its bitterness to the havoc and ruin of death. There is a goodness which is formal, precise and groovy, there is a goodness, too, which is slap-dash and solid, and both of these are excellent of their kind, but there is a goodness also which is one of *nuance* and distinction, a goodness of fragrance and aroma, the goodness of nobly-natured women for the most part—a divine endowment or instinct to some extent perhaps, but also, to some extent, within our own power to cultivate or to ignore. Even man, clumsy, heavy-booted man, may gain a little of this goodness, if he tread warily, and live humbly, and conquer self, and seek to master the language and the signs of love. Emotion and reason must go hand in hand; head and heart be allied in a common service. For there is a soul of reason in the deepest love, and the prayer "Give us knowledge, understanding and discernment," has a fuller meaning than perhaps we are at first sight aware of. As there are those who, living in the same environment and under the same circumstances, find life interesting, and others who find it dull, so there are some who will find opportunities for goodness, where others will pass by with ears that cannot hearken and eyes that cannot see.

There is, then, an intellectual element in goodness. And, lastly, there is an important inter-action between goodness and wisdom. If by wise thought and delicate perception and vivid imagination we may avoid needless pain and find opportunity for positive good, so is it also true that a pure life and a pure love will increase the sharpness of our moral vision.

Here again the widespread tenets of divers philosophies suggest humble applications for our everyday life. We know how some have taught that the highest wisdom is only open to those who are masters in morality, and how others have insisted that the utmost purity of life, rising even in our eyes to unqualified asceticism, is the necessary prelude for the attainment of a spiritual insight into reality.

We have observed that we can only oppose goodness to wisdom by an unreal abstraction, inasmuch as an element of reason enters into all human goodness, but, with this reserve, it is true to say that goodness, on its own field and territory, can see further, and see more truly, than the mere intelligence which is divorced from moral worth. Goodness, as we saw, can be allied to the deepest ignorance, and we shall always proudly maintain that such goodness is both more acceptable to God and more akin to Him than the profoundest knowledge and the most brilliant genius when wedded to a selfish or immoral life. In a notable passage in his "Republic," Plato speaks of the character of a good physician and a good judge, and he urges that the "judge should not be young: he should have learnt to know evil not from his own soul, but from late and long observation of the nature of evil in others; for vice," he says, "cannot know virtue too, but a virtuous nature, educated by time, will acquire a knowledge both of virtue and vice." There is a divine world of beauty into which the vicious man can never enter, the laws of which he cannot discern; in that realm the stupidest servant of goodness, the dullest menial of love, is wiser than he. You cannot do the works of goodness by sheer intelligence;

it is love which must primarily suggest the details of love's service.

> 'Tis Love must see them, as the eye sees light:
> Day is but Number to the darkened sight.

Love can open the eyes of reason: but reason cannot command love.

And so we seem to see that this goodness which shall help wisdom to find the opportunities for adding to its own store, is allied to, if it is not identical with, that warmer, more emotional goodness of which we spoke before. How inter-connected and intertwined with each other all the elements of a full and great personality assuredly are! It struck me when I had got thus far in the analysis of my subject that here was a fitting conclusion for a sermon, because it might be truly said that the glow and passion of goodness may be stirred and stimulated by religion. I thought how the love of God might quicken that love of good which is so sorely needed to keep our poor intelligence on the alert in the service of goodness and in the service of love. And then I remembered how it might also be truly said that the love of

God was itself the creation of the love of man, the love of the visible and the human generating and vitalising the love of the invisible and Divine.

What, then, is the conclusion of the whole matter? It is that the entire man, reason, will and feeling, are all required in the service of goodness. Mind and heart and soul must contribute their quota and their share, while Love, compassing earth and heaven in its range, just because it may not stop short before God, is the better able to recognise, as alone it can, the greatness and lovability of man. For Love is still the Lord of all.

RELIGION AND MORALITY.

" The Lord is righteous; he loves righteousness: the upright shall behold his face." [1]

THE precise relation of religion to morality is a problem for philosophy to elaborate and determine. But that the one is closely connected with the other is a truth which is now happily familiar to us all, and which is common to all the creeds. That the love of God is best expressed by the love of man, that the righteous Lord loves righteousness, that the moral law is the true law of God—these are affirmations which sound to us like the simplest and most obvious truisms. Indeed,

---

[1] Psalm xi. 7 (R.V.).

so simple and obvious do they sound and seem, that we forget not only the long struggles of the past by which they won their way to triumph, not only the many obscurations which have covered and marred their brilliancy, but sometimes even the fact that these mere truisms are vital truths. And yet on the strength and purity of their application depends the degree of excellence and value to which our own lives may severally attain. It was in all probability a long, long while before man permanently connected the Divine power without Him, whose favour he sought and whose wrath he feared, with moral conceptions, and the earlier intimations of that connection were far removed from the precision and comprehensiveness of the pregnant utterance, "God is righteous, and loves righteousness." But the statement of the text is, nevertheless, to some extent, common to all the greater and more historical religions of the world. Haltingly and imperfectly expressed, it has been the element in all of them which has constituted their best truest and Divinest feature, and we may measure their value and gauge the inspiration of their founders and teachers by the purity and intensity with which this truth—the essential and permanent connection of religion and morality with each other—has been grasped and absorbed. Every religious reformation, not only of the past, but also of the present, is always a reassertion in one form or another, and in one application or another, of the Psalmist's dictum, "God is righteous, and loves righteousness."

The largest contributors to the establishment of this dictum were unquestionably the Hebrew prophets. It was they who identified the service of God with the service of goodness, and who in the barest and boldest manner overthrew the religion of rite and ceremonial for the religion of righteousness and compassion. The truth which more or less distinctly has been discerned and taught by the religious and moral exponents of every civilised and semi-civilised people, the truth which is most common and vital to all religions of to-day, the truth which shall go far to constitute by itself the wider Theism of the future, this general truth is also most specifically Jewish. It is the great dogma of Judaism. The assertion that there is one God, and one God only, would be barren and profitless without the qualification which gives this assertion its practical value and import, which relates it to our thoughts, our actions and our hopes. The one God is righteous, and loves righteousness. And in passing, let me here add that when you who have attempted a reform in the outward worship of God, and—what is far more—have asserted that there is a spiritual Judaism higher, more permanent, more satisfying, above all, more *true* than the Judaism of precept and ritual tradition—when, I say, you are told that you are eviscerating Judaism, that you are removing from it what is distinctive and peculiar, and reducing it to *mere* Theism, as if, indeed, Theism were adequately qualified by "*mere*," it were well for you to remember that your empty and eviscerated Judaism is directly based upon the teaching of Amos, Hosea, and Isaiah, and that there can surely be no greater boast and pride for a religion than the consciousness of claiming as its own chosen and characteristic possession that general doctrine which is the common element of truth in all religions of the present, and which of the religion of the future shall be, with all its far reaching implications, well-nigh the substance and the sum.

To-day, however, I desire, for a few moments, to consider the second part of the Psalmist's utterance, which is really an inseparable portion of it. In the Authorised Version, as in the Greek and Latin renderings, the words are mis-translated. The Revised Version has the correct translation: "The upright shall behold His face." Similarly in the close of the 140th Psalm, it is said "The righteous shall give thanks unto Thy name; the upright shall dwell in Thy presence."

The righteous then shall see God. It is of course obvious that the words are not to be taken literally. The vision of God is a vision to the inner or spiritual sense: it is the righteous who shall realise God, who shall commune with Him. "The secret of the Lord is with them that fear Him." It is like which understands like. The righteous God is grasped by the righteous man. Sins separate from God; goodness brings near to Him; through morality to religion.

To enable man to realise God, even to feel God, has been the aim of practical religion in all ages. It was attempted sensuously long before it was attempted spiritually. The desire to draw near to the Divine, or to draw the Divine down to the human level, lies very possibly at the origin of sacrifice. It was one of the sources of magic and sorcery. It suggested the whole fabric of religious ceremonial. It lies at the bottom of all theories of mediation and incarnation.

The Psalmists also experienced the desire to draw near to God, nor did they disdain the use of material bridges or intermediaries. The defenders of religious ceremonial, the upholders of public worship, may appeal to them for illustration and support. But their fundamental method is independent of adventitious aid. Paraphrasing and enlarging it, we may say that it is the Divine element in man—the incarnation, if you please, of a fragment of the Divine Spirit within each human frame—by which man discerns and realises God. But this is not all. It is not sufficient for human reason to apprehend the Divine reason: such an intellectual apprehension could produce no religious communion between God and man. It is reason in the form of goodness, reason transfigured into love, which alone discerns and realises the essence of the Divine nature, discerns it as goodness, realises it as love.

Is this mere vague, tall talk? I think it is difficult, but not vague; it is arduous truth, but not mere vapid rhodomontade. We are, of course, dealing with impalpable feelings and with spiritual realities. They can be talked about, but cannot be proved. There is but one and the same world for the dullard and the poet, for the Atheist and the Theist. The difference lies in the interpretation. There is also a scale in the power of spiritual apprehension. Some people are more religious than others. By this I do not mean that the more religious people are necessarily morally better than the others; that would be inaccurate, and inaccuracy in the long run does not help religion or any other cause. Nor do I mean that the others are intellectually less certain of the existence of God, or that they observe fewer rites and ceremonies; they may indeed observe far more. I mean that some people live more habitually in the full presence of God than others, and are more helped forward in the path of duty by religious motives. To some people duty and the will of God are inseparably joined, while God's will is but another term for God's love. Yet such people live the same sort of lives as those who find it very hard to "draw near unto God," as the author of the 73rd Psalm puts it, very hard to say truthfully, "I am continually with Thee." Still, all who can say honestly, "I believe in God," however unable they may be to give any intelligible explanation of their belief, may be helped to some degree by the dictum of the Psalmist, "The upright shall behold God's face."

First of all, though the doctrine taught is stern, severe and simple, it is for that very reason bracing, stimulative, ennobling.

We are to find God by doing our duty. We are not to find Him primarily in a book, or in doctrine, or in rites, or in contemplation, but by action. This seems to deprive us of many valuable media between ourselves and God, but it does not really deprive us of them. It only puts them in their fit subsidiary place. In their proper order we may use them, but not before. The good God is to be found by goodness. Narrow your conception of duty, conventionalise your conception of goodness, and your vision of God will be narrow and conventional too. It is, we may suppose, no mere negative uprightness which will bestow upon us the prerogative of beholding God's face. There are only two sorts of people, I imagine—please think for yourselves whether I am right or not, for I am only feeling my way—there are only two sorts of people who find goodness and duty easy. The first sort is made up of people whose goodness is meagre, customary, unsubstantial—people who take life easily, or at all events who take purity and devotion and sacrifice and conscientiousness easily, and do not trouble much about them—average folk in a word, a class to which most of us belong, if not always, at least on five days out of the seven. But the moral consciousness of man in all ages and lands has not been hopelessly astray in saying in a thousand different ways, "hard is the good"; and thus, if goodness be hard, and through goodness we come to God, it is not easy to find Him. The person who, because his goodness is feeble finds goodness easy, will hardly have more than a feeble grasp upon God; he will see but little of His face, and will see that little seldom.

There is indeed another sort of people who find goodness easy or seem to find it so. They form a very small class—small and select. They are "the saints that are on the earth," who have worked their way up to God, or having set God always before them, cannot be moved. And some, too, there are, women rather than men, who seem to have never forgotten the Divine source whence their souls have sprung:

> Not in entire forgetfulness,
> And not in utter nakedness,
> But trailing clouds of glory do they come
> From God, who is their home.

But these, possessed, as it would seem to the outsider, of a Divine instinct for purity and goodness, are very few in number, and perhaps they too have known their times of conflict and of trial. In the long run and as a nearly universal rule, it holds true of moral excellence as of artistic and intellectual excellence: "hard is the good."

Is it not then a bracing doctrine that the upright may behold God's face? If the struggle be hard, the reward is high. Many of us in some moments of endeavour or of sacrifice, of fortitude in adversity, or constancy in temptation, may have had a glimpse of God. The veil will be lifted more, as we aspire more, and achieve more. We shall not only realise God more often, but realise Him as He is in spite of evil. That will be a better and fuller realisation than external reminders. It will be an inward experience. That God is, we may accept by reason; what God is, we must realise by love. Once more: through morality to religion, through goodness to God.

Again, if the doctrine of the Psalmist be severe, it is also general. "Hard is the good"; but yet, unlike excellence in intellect or beauty, moral excellence lies within the reach—if the search for it be not too long delayed—of every ordinary mortal. There is no reason therefore why the vision of God, which is conditional on goodness, should be limited to a few.

Lastly, the doctrine is very valuable at the present time. It does not, indeed, preclude the advent of those intellectual and moral difficulties which make the idea of God, in the ordinary sense of the word, very difficult to accept. Nor does it solve these difficulties, least of all the purely intellectual ones. But it does help towards the endurance, if not towards the intellectual comprehension of evil. Has it not been a remarkable fact that in all ages and creeds the very people who have loved God most have had the keenest sense for human misery? And yet this misery, which, after all, look at it how you will, is suffered, if not ordered to exist, by Omnipotence, has not extinguished their love of God, but rather quickened it to a brighter flame. Take such a man as St. Francis of Assisi. He certainly realised both the wretchedness of man *and* the goodness of God more keenly than his contemporaries, and the one perception seemed but to accentuate the other. Again, even self-experienced misery has been powerless to quench man's capacity to love God. The explanations of the misery have been often wholly untenable, but while the explanations have varied, the essential faith has remained the same. In spite and in the midst of evil men have clung to God. Human love has opened their eyes to Divine love. And so for us, if we are oppressed by the endless and hopeless horrors of the present and the past, so that faith in God becomes very hard and difficult, the solution seems to be, not to know and learn less of life, but to know and learn still more. For moral, as well as for intellectual difficulties, the advice of a great teacher—I have, I fancy, quoted it to you before—holds good: "At the worst, live on as if there were God and duty, and they will prove themselves to you in your life." If we see insufficient evidence to make us believe in Divine goodness and Divine love, this may be because we have not shown and learnt and acquired sufficient human goodness and human love ourselves. Increase the quantity and the quality of these, and the inference will become to most of us irresistible: more inexplicable than evil with God is love without God. Through morality to religion, through goodness to God.

Thus our Psalmist's doctrine is, to some extent at least, helpful towards a spiritual, though not an intellectual, solution of some of the primal difficulties which lie at the root and basis of all religion. But it is still more helpful for the difficulties which are less primary and essential, but which, nevertheless, press heavy upon many a soul and seem more gruesome and more important than in truth they are. "The upright shall behold God's face." The upright in this life on earth shall realise God. That truth, if truth it be, is quite independent of criticism; whether Moses wrote the Pentateuch, or whether he did not write a single line of it, makes not the smallest difference to us in the process and in the achievement of realising God. It will neither hasten nor retard our communion with Him. I do not want to exaggerate the *non*-importance of criticism, for I hold that it must affect some of the dogmas of orthodox Judaism and must ultimately very seriously affect its outer form and embodiment. But to exaggerate its importance is a far more serious evil. Depend upon it the real religion of the individual, his personal consciousness of God, his personal communion with Him, his perception of the Divine goodness, are absolutely unaffected by all the historical criticism in the world. That consciousness, that communion, that perception, as they are found and maintained by spiritual and moral methods, are not to be lost except by moral lassitude or spiritual decay.

The scientific investigation of written documents stands outside their sphere, and neither invalidates their certitude nor dulls the capacity by which to apprehend them. So, too, with miracles. If an angel from heaven came down to say either that all the miracles of the Bible are true, or that miracles are inconsistent with the Divine nature, in neither case would the gradient of our ascent to God be altered or the direction of our pathway be changed. The measure of difficulty would not be increased or diminished; still would the upright, and still the upright only, behold God's face. With the miracles or without them, the fundamental dogma of Judaism remains the same: through morality to religion, through goodness to God.

Am I making an inaccurate and exaggerated statement in claiming the dictum of the Psalmist, thus expanded and understood, as a fundamental dogma of Judaism? I do not think so. We are accustomed to hear that Judaism lays more stress on works than faith, on doing than profession. Such statements are liable to mislead, but it would be true to say that Judaism from the time of the prophets onwards has linked religion and morality indissolubly together, and urged that the religious life must, as it were, be expressed in moral terms. The later ceremonialism of the law obscured the simpler, truer, and more purely moral teaching of the prophets, but the conviction that only goodness leads Godwards was always maintained. And at the present time, when ceremonialism is waning, the maxim, "The righteous shall see God," is acknowledged on all hands. The moral to be drawn from it, indeed, is less controversial than spiritual. Only they, perhaps, who have sought through righteousness to see God have the right and the power to work at religious reform. The one must logically precede the other, although practically they may have to go hand in hand. We must, indeed strive that the outward forms and embodiment of Judaism which have come down to us from the historic past, shall gradually be moulded into fuller accordance with our actual ideas, beliefs and aspirations; but beyond and before all these things we must seek to qualify ourselves to live up to the level of that spiritual Judaism in the reality and all-sufficiency of which we profess to believe. This sounds a bit conceited, but I mean it humbly enough.

We must seek God in our own hearts and by our own lives before and while we attempt to worship Him with worthier forms, in public halls and synagogues. *How* we must seek, and how, seeking, we may hope to find Him, we have already learnt. Private prayer in such a shape and after such a fashion as suits best each individual, is also a means which can only be ignored or interrupted with danger and detriment. But the most essential means has been indicated to us by the dictum of the Psalmist: "The upright shall behold God's face." Be pure, steadfast, honest; be eager in well-doing, willing in sacrifice, brave in danger, resolute in temptation; be—but what needs say more? Do not most of us know where and how we could live better lives, purer lives, fuller, stronger, more useful lives than now we do?

Do not most of us know the skeleton in our own moral cupboard? Could we not all put to a more searching test than hitherto the truth and reality of our axiom: Through morality to religion, through goodness to God?

THE CONSCIOUSNESS OF JUDAISM.

"In thee shall all the families of the earth be blessed." [1]

THESE famous words in the call and blessing of Abraham are, in all probability, mistranslated. The true rendering is: "In, or with thee all the families of the earth shall bless themselves." Thus the universalist meaning, which has been expounded and emphasised on countless occasions from countless pulpits, is a misapprehension, however excellent, of the original text. All that the original writer meant to convey was that other nations should desire for

---

[1] Genesis xii. 3.

themselves the same blissful good fortune which was promised to the seed of Abraham. Nevertheless the Greek and Aramaic translators both accepted the other and universalist explanation, and largely through their influence this grander rendering has come to be the one which is most widely and popularly adopted. Of the three most famous Jewish commentators in the Middle Ages, two have given it the sanction of their authority, and in modern times it has been dwelt upon with peculiar pride and satisfaction by almost every Jewish preacher.

In this verse, then, we have a notable example how in the course of ages—for some 600 years lay between the composition of the twelfth chapter of Genesis and its Greek translation—a wider or more catholic interpretation was read into the original text. Other instances could be given where a reverse process has taken place, and where the more liberal or universalist meaning of the original has been narrowed and degraded by the erroneous explanations of a later age. And in these curious facts we may see, as in a figure, the constant alternation of attitude of the Jewish people and the Jewish religion towards the big outer world which lies beyond their pale.

Both the poles of this alternative were caused by religion. It was religion which caused that bitter and violent nationalism, producing in its turn that consciousness of perfect harmony between its own cause and the cause of God, which has been imitated with cruel and mournful consequences by many another people down even to our own age. It was religion, on the other hand, which caused that conception of the Jewish people as the servant of the nations, as entrusted with a mission for the benefit of mankind, upon which modern Jewish orators often dwell with keen satisfaction and pride, albeit they seldom attempt to show how the mission is being, or is to be, accomplished. It was religion which induced a Talmudic Rabbi to say that the whole object of the Jewish dispersion was the making of proselytes, just as it was religion, although a narrow and perverted religion, which induced another Rabbi to say that proselytes were a misfortune to Israel. On the one hand religion merely tended to strengthen the purely human feelings of national solidarity and pride, and to invest them with a mistaken sanction of spurious divinity; on the other, by its truly divine power, and in virtue of the Holy Spirit of God which was working in and through human instruments and organs, it broke through and tore asunder this integument of national self-glory and national hate, and soared again and again to noble expressions of universalism and liberality.

By the most developed theologian of the Hebrew Scriptures—I mean the second or Babylonian Isaiah—the universalist doctrine is most strongly marked, and while in the age of Ezra a contrary direction set in, yet that same age witnessed in all probability the production of those two exquisite writings, polemical pamphlets in the cause of universalism as they really are, though their teaching has become obscured by the art of their authors—Jonah and Ruth. And with the generation which succeeded Ezra the era of proselytism began.

So the two opposite tendencies continue, the

irony of circumstance tending mainly and in the long run to help and foster the separatist and national instincts, while yet the other and wider view, the view which regards the Jews as a religious brotherhood and only accidentally as a peculiar race, ever and anon broke and penetrated through the obstructions whether of internal prejudice or of external persecution, and in the darkest ages of our history was never entirely lost or utterly without its prophet and its witness.

And at the present day, in spite of the unfortunate recrudescence of shameful persecution, and the consequent temporary recrudescence of a waning nationalism, the catholic interpretation of Judaism is slowly but surely gaining ground. It is being recognised that the Jews as a religious brotherhood have some religious relation, some definite duty to the world beyond, even if that duty be at present one of mere silence and aloofness.

And if Judaism as a community is charged with this duty, then also is the individual Jew. For the community, if something more than the sum of its members, is nevertheless composed of them. Whatever then be the mission of Judaism to the outer world, whether it is to teach religious truth by isolation or to teach it by attraction, whether it is to help the world by ignoring it or to help it by the offer of a share in its own spiritual possessions, a full participation in its own religious embodiment, whether it is to diffuse Judaism by maintaining its national characteristics, or to diffuse it by gradually effacing them—in either case and in any variety of each alternative (and these are endless) the issue depends on the individuals who compose it. Upon our shoulders, congregants, falls the duty; upon us lies the responsibility. Nay, even if you honestly believe that Judaism has no present duty to the world beyond, no interest in the nations except that there may be always enough Gentiles to light the fires of the elect, even then, circumscribed though your vision may be, Judaism still bears a duty to itself. Fidelity to Judaism, as we each of us conceive it, this is the indispensable condition to the success of its mission, whatever that mission may be. Fidelity to Judaism, as you conceive it, this is the stern corollary of your acceptance of its name. So long as each individual can still honestly say, "I believe in Judaism," whatever sense he may attach to the word, so long is he bound to regard and to fulfil the responsibilities of his belief.

It is tolerably obvious that even as people's conception of Judaism and of its relation to the world is exceedingly various, so, or little less varying, must also be their conception of how they best can show fidelity to its cause. And I regard it as very important that this diversity of conception and of method should be fully recognised and appreciated. It is very important that the keen consciousness of Judaism should not be appropriated by any one section of the community. The progress of Judaism depends not on attempting to make all Jews think alike, or on laying down the limits within which a Jew remains a Jew, but in seeking to secure and heighten the religious consciousness of being a Jew in the widest possible number of persons. We may take it for granted that no one will desire to call himself a Jew who is in any legitimate sense a Christian, a Mahommedan, or a Buddhist. Within this limit the man who seeks to live the religious life with the consciousness of being a Jew must find his legitimate place in the Jewish camp whether he conforms to my and your conception of Judaism or whether he departs from it.

It is commonly said that there is a tendency among Jews to become less Jewish in the sunshine of prosperity. When Israel waxes fat, he kicks. There is a certain amount of obvious truth in this complaint. In all ages and in all religious communities, the blood of martyrs has been the seed of the Church. But seeing that the essence of the Jewish religion lies in the immense stress which it lays upon the moral life on earth, as the truest exemplification of our belief in and love of God, I am not wholly prepared to say that we are less Jewish now than we were fifty years ago, unless it can also be proved we are less moral. So far as we are that, so far as we are more selfish and proud, more greedy of money and advancement, more material and coarse, less spiritual and less chaste, than our ancestors of fifty years ago, so far emphatically have we degenerated in our Judaism, and by so much were they better Jews than we.

There are two main methods—and neither can be neglected without some peril both to the individual and to the community—by which fidelity to Judaism can be displayed. The first method is chiefly (though not exclusively) shown in a constant and habitual participation in the outward religious life and outward religious embodiment of the community as such. The most obvious instance of this participation is attendance at public worship. Secondly, there is the moral life, lived with conscious intent and desire, in every section of our lives, not only in our homes but in our occupations, professions and trades, and there is also the inner life of the spirit, the life of prayer, self-sacrifice and love. There is the conscious expression of religion in terms of morality; and the constant carrying up of morality to its source and its seat in the love of God. This, also, is a Jewish method, for this intermingling of religion and morality, so that each is strengthened and purified by the other, is characteristically Jewish.

But perhaps some one will say that to characterise this method as Jewish is to be guilty of arrogance. Is morality or religiousness, it may be asked, the exclusive possession of the Jews? And in this objection, though quite honestly made, a great danger, as I think, lurks unseen. Who would deny that other creeds also teach and practise religiousness and morality? But that which is a quality of one creed may be also a quality of another. If I could magically detect the three best men and the three best women in this synagogue, and compel them by my wizardry to step forward publicly together, we should find that some of the most admirable and distinctive qualities of the first were shared by one or more of their fellows. But shall we say that because, for example, the humility of A is matched and equalled by the humility of B, therefore humility is not a special characteristic and a peculiar grace of either B or A? To lie is un-English, says the Englishman, and I hope with truth; to lie is un-German, says the German, and I hope he too is here no liar. May we therefore not claim truth as part of the Englishman's character and as parcel of his national creed?

The objection is, therefore, to my thinking, groundless. But it is also dangerous. There are a large number of persons in our midst who are commonly called non-observant Jews. Now I do not wish to protect or excuse these persons, although I am aware that, judged by a certain standard, I should be regarded as a non-observant Jew myself. But using the words roughly, I notice a double tendency: first, the observer is inclined to think that the non-observer is not a Jew. Secondly, the non-observer is also inclined to think that the observer's judgment of him is correct.

Now, speaking generally, the observant Jew who also strives to live this full moral and religious life of which I spoke before, is a more perfect Jew than he who lives the life but is wholly non-observant. Religion, too, needs its embodiment, and I am seriously inclined to believe that several generations of non-observance would result in a decay of inward religiousness and a weakening of outward morality. Nevertheless, it will be acknowledged on all hands that the more important part of a man's religion, the more important part, therefore, I do not hesitate to say, of a Jew's Jewish religion, is the moral life which he leads and the moral and religious character which he is.

Now, this being so, I will venture to say that Judaism would not be harmed, but, on the contrary, would be materially benefited, if *both* the observer *and* the non-observer would recognise that he who accepts the essentials of the Jewish creed and lives up to them, who loves God and seeks to express that love in his life, who tries to do God's will on earth, as in his home, so also in his daily work and occupation,—that such a person is not only a good man, but in the most essential elements of our religion, a good Jew, and doing yeoman service to the Jewish cause.

For the strict observer, if he recognises and realises this truth, will be less downcast in his estimate of our religious future, and, may I add, he will perhaps also be somewhat less self-satisfied in his own religious condition. He will seek to make the nobility of his life and the beauty of his character rival and equal the rigidity of his observance, and thus to increase the number of those whom we have already recognised as the most perfect members of our faith, in whom the outward and inward life of religion are in serene and flawless harmony with one another. He will not abandon the attempt to make the non-observant Jew more observant, but he will do this, not on the assumption that the man who holds to our conception of God and his service, and leads a noble life, is only a good man, but not yet a good Jew, but on the assumption that he is indeed a good Jew, though not a perfect one, that he must above all things be recognised as a member of our brotherhood and encouraged to maintain and to realise his Jewish consciousness and his Jewish faith.

And no less important is the change of attitude and view which the full acceptance of my theory should have upon the non-observer, or upon him whose observance is slack and whose links of connection with our community are snapping asunder. It must, I think, help to claim him as one of us, to keep him within our camp, a soldier of God fighting the good fight under the banner of our Jewish faith. If it is generally admitted and recognised that the noble character and the noble life built up upon the basis, and recruited from the power of the Jewish creed is seven-eighths of Judaism, the consciousness of being, and the desire to be and remain a Jew will be widened in area and intensified in degree. The man who now hardly regards himself as a Jew may then perhaps be proud of his Judaism, and find in it a strength, a solace and reality of which he had never dreamed before.

Let me try to put what I mean more correctly and simply before you in the following way. Take a busy doctor and busy barrister who are non-observing Jews. Remember that we have already laid down the principle that they would be more perfect Jews if they were observant, but as a matter of fact they are not. I will not argue whether they could or ought to observe more than they do. Personally, I have had no temptation not to observe as much as seems to me to square with my own conception of Judaism, and no practical difficulties in doing so. Therefore I am an incompetent judge to decide their cause. But no pressure of work or complication of circumstance can prevent those men from trying to love God and to do His will, to honour and search for truth, and to maintain that vital interconnection between religion and morality, practice and belief, in which the dominant note of Judaism consists. They can be believing and professing Jews through seven-eighths of the area over which the Jewish religion extends. For the sake of Judaism, as well as for your sake and for theirs, I bid you encourage and strengthen them in the consciousness of their Judaism, I bid you assure them that the more fully and consistently they live as in the presence of God, the more they are forwarding the cause of Judaism, promoting its development, and hastening its triumph. So best shall you help to keep them Jews, conscious and proud of their Jewish faith, and of the religious brotherhood to which they belong, anxious to maintain their Judaism, and keen to purify, develop and diffuse it.

Once more, if these men become more conscious that they are Jews and are regarded as such, will not the need come to them too to take more active part in the outward religious life of the community, and to join more frequently in its public worship of God? The outward embodiment of religion is slowly but surely subject to variation and change. What is needed is that, as far as possible, it should be in harmony with the inward religion of the largest number of its adherents. When the need comes to those who are now so largely outsiders to have a ceremonial religion as well as a moral and spiritual religion, they will take their part with us in securing that this ceremonial shall best answer to the needs of the largest number of worshippers. So long as men stay away from public worship they can hardly complain if the services of the synagogue are arranged to suit the men and women who attend, rather than those who neglect them.

Is what I have said of a purely destructive tendency? Have I made the way easy to indifference and desertion? Surely not. How glad should I be if the seats in this synagogue were crowded, both upstairs and downstairs, Saturday after Saturday. But are we likely to attain this desirable end by mere admonition or entreaty? I think not. Yet in going another way to work I have not gone a way of comfort and of ease. The religious life, in the sense already defined, the religious life which is expressed and realised in noble character and noble deed, is emphatically not easy. But who amongst you will dare to say either that it is not a Jewish life, or that it is antiquated or impossible under the conditions in which we live? Is love antiquated? Is truth antiquated? Is God antiquated? Then is Judaism not antiquated. Religion—it is the doctrine of

Judaism—must be wrought out in the world, manifested in this life, even though this life be but the preparation for another. Is there not room in every life for sacrifice to duty and sacrifice to truth? Cannot the man of business live more honestly, the employer care more for his workmen, the master for his servant, the servant for his master? If there is room for better knowledge and better life here, then is there still room for devotion to the cause of Judaism. A distinguished Christian divine is reported to have said to wavering outsiders, "If you cannot come to us with the miracles, then in God's name come to us without them." May I not with better reason say to our wavering outsiders: "If you cannot come to us with the forms, then in God's name come to us without them." Know yourselves as Jews, love God, live the highest life you can, and you will learn to feel the need of forms from within. Then shall a valuable Judaism of religious symbolism and of outward form be gradually added on to the still higher and truer Judaism of your faith, your character and your lives. For he is not a

Jew who is one outwardly, nor is that Judaism which is of the letter only ; but he is a Jew who is one inwardly, and who seeks, so far as human frailty will permit him, to live and to work in the realised presence of God.

www.ingramcontent.com/pod-product-compliance
Lightning Source LLC
Chambersburg PA
CBHW032133230426
43672CB00011B/2319